"Emily Edwards brings well-worn subject of dating. With a .... experience, practical wisdom, and scriptural support, she lays out an immensely helpful roadmap for preparing for marriage. I highly, highly recommend it!"

— DWIGHT EDWARDS, **Author of** *Revolution Within*,
a direct descendant of the renowned early-American
preacher Jonathan Edwards

"*Ready and Waiting* is a very powerful and hard-hitting book that really gets to the heart of the spiritual issues that we all face in our lives. If we can just take a moment or two and be intellectually honest enough to put our preconditioned ideas and biases about personal relationships to the side, and give this book a fair reading, we will find that our hearts and minds can truly be blessed, challenged, and changed. I encourage you today as you explore this book to apply all truth personally and be "Ready and Waiting" to see what God will do for your good and His glory. Keep looking up!"

— REV. JIM LAKE, **Author of** *From the Pen of the Poet to the Beat of the Heart*

"*Ready and Waiting* expertly focuses on how to live life through Christ whether single, dating, or in a committed relationship. Emily offers insight for singles and couples demonstrating that each phase of life is part of God's plan, and each phase has its own blessings."

— MELISSA MARSAC

"Yes, ladies and gentlemen, we are different, but Edwards defines and outlines how we can make these differences work with one another. Through her examples, steps, and advice, Edwards illustrates that with successful communication and forgiveness, we can experience contentment with God and others."

— SARA SCHROEDER

"Emily Edwards carefully crafts her words into a literary gem for her readers...carrying them from singleness, through dating, into marriage, and beyond! Her constant appeal to the Word of God as the supreme authority in life, and the Person of Jesus Christ as the ultimate hope and divine Lover of our souls, is refreshing. She poises her readers for relational success on all levels by pointing them first to the Son of God to find their deepest hungers glutted and their deepest thirsts slaked, and then (and only then) turns them out to love others radically in the power of His Spirit."

— DAVID SHOWALTER

"While reading *Ready and Waiting*, I felt the conviction of the Holy Spirit, and I e-mailed my husband to show my willingness to work on an issue with him. I absolutely loved the humor in the book. I caught myself smiling or laughing more than once. Additionally, I can see this book being required reading for couples having premarital counseling."

— NAN SNIPES

"Emily conveys deep and insightful truths about the differences between men and women in a clear and understandable way. Reading her book will revolutionize the way that you view the opposite sex."

— CALEB WEATHERL

"Reading Emily's book left me more thankful for my singleness than I've ever been. It also opened my eyes to the ways God can use me uniquely during this time."

— ELIZABETH YORK

Austin,
May God fill your
heart with love,
and bless you
always!
Emily Edwards

Ready & Waiting

A Biblical Approach to
Singleness, Dating,
and Preparation for Marriage

EMILY A. EDWARDS, PH.D.

Living Hope Publishing • Midland, Texas

LIVING HOPE PUBLISHING
P.O. Box 2153
Midland, TX 79702
www.LivingHopePublishing.com

Cover and interior design © TLC Graphics, www.TLCGraphics.com
Cover: Tamara Dever; Interior: Erin Stark

ISBN 13: 978-0-9816709-0-4
Library of Congress Control Number: 2008906234

Table of Contents

Acknowledgments

First and foremost I would like to thank my Lord and Savior, Jesus Christ. You are "my rock and my fortress and my deliverer; my God, my strength, in whom I will trust" (Psalm 18:2 NKJV). Thank you, Lord, for blessing me with the gift of everlasting life. Thank you for Your unending grace, love, patience, and kindness towards me. Thank you for being the greatest example of love I know.

Much appreciation goes to my editor, Heidi Nigro, who is not only bright and talented, but absolutely has been a joy to work with. Thank you so much for your invaluable feedback and suggestions, which have added significant improvements and clarity to this book.

My deepest thanks also go to my family: Charles and Frances Younger, Ben-David and Bridgette Edwards, Ryan and Leah Johnerson, Katie Younger, Meredith Younger, Tom Younger, Dave and Betty Anderson, Wayne and Jackie Dunkel, Jim and Donna Harris, Sandy Edwards, Steve and Carrilynn Fontenot, Laura Anderson, Jimmy Anderson, Scott and Christy Funderburk, Mark Anderson, John Dunkel, Luke Dunkel, Jonathan Harris, Joshua Harris, Stephen Edwards, Jordan Edwards, Brandon Edwards, Eric Fontenot, Marie Fontenot, and the others I love so much.

My deep thanks and gratitude also go out to my friends: Vince and Gail Loftis, David Crass, Amye Crass, Tom and Susan Voskamp, Kathleen Utsman, Keith and Christy Petty, Cletus and Beci Amstutz, Dr. Fred Lybrand, Tom and Dana Beard, Tyler and Shannon Beard, Jeff and Rachel Beard, Dave and Barbara Daupert,

Kyle and Jamie Stallings, Rhett and Janice Gist, Buddy and Holly Gieb, Tad and Margo Hillin, Stephen and Jovita Lambert, Whitney Good, Kyle and Tara Jones, Grant and Michelle Wright, Cutler Gist, Hilary Posey, Randi Froman, Julene Haggard, Brenda Davis, Jon Morgan, John and D'Ann Norwood, Dora Duarte, Eric Boyt, Trey Walker, Renea Wells, Lolly Avila, Elizabeth York, Nan Snipes, Craig and Darla Taylor, Stan and Deborah Fikes, Tim and Terri Dunn, Hermann and Louise Eben, Jim and Ruth Hughes, Tim and Amy Leach, Cami McCurdy, Debbie McCurdy, Regina Kuethe, Cheryl Lyons, John Williams, Jim and Edna Lake, Ray and Ruth Fairbank, Ralph Miller, Heidi Dobey, Clint Alderman, Craig Stanfield, David Showalter, Jessica Dority, Laurie Southwick, Sheryl Nobley, Jodi Weidmark, Fred and Valerie Paine, Erik and Bambi Carlson, Sandra Tarlen, Ted Sellers, Norma Godshall, Dianne Kazenski, David and Suzanne Ritzenthaler, Mark and Sue Ford, Rocky and LuAnn Nystrom, Matt Nystrom, Kyle and Whitney Groves, Don McGee, Kathy Sandusky, Melissa Bramley, Brandy Bell, Michele Greene, Dwight Edwards, Jack and Donna Abraham, Bruce and Martha Lowe, Sunni Hollums, JoAnn Velasquez, Julie Miller, Niki Speicher, Randy and Judy Rouse, Layne and Apple Rouse, Daniel and Kayla Stephens, Jim and Becky Martin, Tom and Susan Vermillion, Larry and Debbie Quinney, Gregg and Kelly Matte, Amy Stephens, Mark Hunter, David and Christine Griffith, Dr. Stan DeKoven, Dr. Tom Leding, Chris Ryden, Caleb Weatherl, Ben Chapman, Arnold and Susan Nall, Don and Susie Evans, Joey and Jan O'Neill, Van and Donna Pearcy, Patrick and Cindy Payton, Freddy and Becky Haltom, David and Betty Mallams, Bobby and Janice Henry, Mark and Colleen McLane, Megan McLane, Wes and Roni Perry, James and Cindy Bobo, Chris and Jenny Craig, Randy and Amy Sims, David and Leslie Smith, Laynce and Leslie Nix, Dr. Roger Traxel, Steve and Debra Weatherl, Cheryl Barker, Deborah Zeck, Andy and Becky Deck, Bryan and Lee Ann Brownfield, Bob and Heidi Fu, David and Annie Day, Dr. Vincent Bash III, Mike and Connie

Acknowledgments

Perrin, Jason and Ruth Schultz, Della Burrow, Leslie Hinton, Tina Strickling, Shan and Lisa Moon, Jack Harper, Lisa Frosch, John and Debbie Chapman, Greg and Emily Yoxsimer, Dr. David and Cindy DeShan, Hector LaChapelle, Avi Ben Yosef, Sara Schroeder, Crista Beattie, Justyn Tappe, and too many more to mention.

Although I have said "thank you" to everyone above, the words themselves do not seem enough to express the heartfelt gratitude that I feel toward each and every one of you. You have all been wonderful, and I am truly grateful for your encouragement and support.

I would like to say "thank you" to those not specifically acknowledged here but who have made a significant difference in my life. Many of you know who you are, but many of you may not even be aware of your positive impact on my life. Some day you will know, even if it's on the other side of the veil. In the meantime, God bless all of you!

Introduction

Dating relationships require much of our time and energy. Oftentimes, our hearts are broken. We long for "the one," as we struggle with waiting. We hope for "the one," as we struggle with dating.

Maybe you are frustrated because you can't find the one for you, no matter how hard you pray. Maybe you have had many relationships, but for some reason, you can't seem to close the deal. Maybe you are afraid of making the same mistakes, or perhaps you have been in a relationship that ended in a negative way. If you could go back, you might do things differently. You might take the time to ask more questions, learn more, grow more, reveal more, and argue less.

There have been times in my dating life when I felt so confused that I thought my brain would explode. I said, "God, either arrange a marriage for me or make me a nun because this dating thing is not working!" We all have those days.

The majority of us date because we want to get married someday. But, instead of striving toward this goal, too many of us are rushing toward it. As we do, we risk making a short-sighted and foolish mistake. Instead of racing to the altar, we should race toward developing a personal and intimate relationship with Jesus Christ. Once we have this firm anchor, then we can safely move forward. We need to make sure that Jesus is number one in our lives instead of the person we are interested in.

My goal in writing this book is to give you a clearer biblical perspective on relationships. Hopefully, what I am about to share will encourage you to "Trust in the Lord with all your heart and lean not on your own understanding" (Proverbs 3:5). It is my sincere desire that you will be able to depend on the Lord for your every need instead of depending on anyone or anything else, and that you will take the time to make sure you are building your relationship on the right foundation before saying, "I do."

This book is not intended to touch on every aspect of dating relationships and preparation for marriage. Rather, it is an outline of the most common relationship hurdles and misunderstandings I've seen in my years as a Christian counselor. It will not solve all of your relationship problems, but it is my hope that it will open your eyes to the challenges, as well as the joys, that await those who are desiring marriage. I hope that it will give you some of the tools you need to get there.

This book is about more than just relationships. It is about the work that God desires to do in you as you wait for that special someone. For those reasons, if I may be so bold as to hope for something more, I pray that this book will motivate you to be all that God desires you to be.

CHAPTER ONE

Party of One

"For I know the plans I have for you," declares the Lord,
"plans to prosper you and not to harm you,
plans to give you hope and a future."

JEREMIAH 29:11

I wonder if our Heavenly Father looks down at some of us and wonders why we are so discontented and why we struggle, whine, and cry so much. I can almost see Him gazing upon me, saying, "I want you to know I loved you so much that I died for you. I have given you the opportunity to have a wonderful, adventurous, and joyful life. Yet, you are not experiencing it. You are continually frustrated and unfulfilled." Or, to put it into language many of us can better identify with: "Get a life! Get a *real* life!"

In this book, my goal is to help you prepare for a healthy, satisfying marriage. Before we get started, however, I want to assure you that the single life can offer contentment, too. In fact, when writing about those who are single or who have been widowed, the apostle Paul wrote, "It is good for them to stay unmarried, as I am" (1 Corinthians 7:8).

"Good" doesn't necessarily mean "preferred," of course. Marriage is designed by God as part of His ordained plan for humanity. This is why many of us struggle with loneliness and frustration as we wait for the right person. The good news is, we don't have to live our lives being down. There is a better way, and it is down on our knees.

1

Are You Incomplete Without Marriage?

Not long ago, I sent an e-mail to a number of single Christians I know, asking them what frustrates them most about the single life and why they think they are not married. The honesty with which they responded was encouraging. As I looked over their answers, I kept seeing two reasons over and over.

The first reason was, "If I get married, life will be perfect. If I am single, life will fall short of perfection." This is a misconception, and a powerful one. Many people rush into marriage because they have a fairy tale image of what marriage should be. They read romance novels, go to weddings, and watch married couples they know, idealizing what they see. In essence, they fall in love with the notion of being married.

These people think, *If I could find a great man or woman, have the perfect wedding, a wonderful honeymoon, a nice home, a good income, a new car, and great children, then everything would be perfect.* But is this really true? If you ask anyone who is married or has been married, they will tell you that it isn't. Marriage isn't easy. Even great marriages experience hard times, and even during the good times, marriage can still be difficult. It is not easy sharing your life, your priorities, and your privacy with another human being (as wonderful as he or she might be) twenty-four hours a day, seven days a week, for the rest of your life. Many people think that, once they get married, many of their problems will be over. In reality, they will merely exchange one set of problems for another.

This is why, in Ephesians 5:15–17, Paul writes, "Be very careful, then, how you live—not as unwise but as wise, making the most of every opportunity, because the days are evil. Therefore do not be foolish, but understand what the Lord's will is." This verse tells me that I should not rush into marriage. I can wait for marriage, but as I do, I don't have to live my life with the pause button pushed. I need to make the most of every day. God wants me to have an abundant life, full of joy and satisfaction. I need to take advantage of the time I am given and make every moment count.

You don't have to live *your* life with the pause button pushed either, thinking that everything is going to get better once you are married. You need to let God use you now, where you are, to impact the lives around you for His glory. You need to address any issues in your own heart to bring yourself in line with His love and His will first, so that when you do get married, you are prepared to face this new set of challenges.

That's easy to say, but not easy to do, right? It is tough to wait when there is so much societal pressure to get married. How many of you have heard at least one of the following from friends, family, or co-workers?

1. "Why are you still single?"
2. "You are so good-looking. I can't believe nobody has snatched you up."
3. "Why don't you have a special someone in your life?"
4. "Your biological clock is ticking."
5. "The minute you stop looking, God will bring you the right person."

Let's face it. Our society puts pressure on single adults to get married. By the time you hit your late twenties, the race is on. If you are still single by the time you hit your thirties, it is as if something is wrong with you. And yet, in 1 Corinthians 7:7 (NLT), Paul says, "I wish everyone could get along without marrying, just as I do. But we are not all the same. God gives some the gift of marriage, and to others He gives the gift of singleness."

Singleness Is a Gift!

Singleness, a gift? Yes! Despite what society tells us, singleness is a gift from God, just as marriage is a gift. When we try to force God, the giver of all gifts, to grant us marriage when *we* desire, rather than when *He* desires, we are stepping into the wrong territory—His! God will give the gift of marriage at His discretion, in His way, and in His time.

When you begin to question why you are not married, you may start to slip into erroneous thinking. For instance, you might rush into a dating relationship (and possibly even marriage) that you know God has not prepared for you. Or you may start to think, *There must be something wrong with me. I must be defective. Nobody wants to marry me.* If these thoughts sound familiar, do you know what you are guilty of doing? Questioning God's love for you.

God's love is unconditional. He loves you as a single person as much as He would a married person. God created you in His image. He lovingly designed you just the way you are. If you are questioning why you are not married, then you are questioning not just His divinely ordained plan and timing, but His perfect love as well.

I know a woman who once struggled with singleness to the point that it began to define her. She was a successful professional, smart and attractive, and yet, she was nearing thirty years old and her dating life had been a failure. All of her other hopes and dreams began to take a backseat to her quest to find a husband. Her prayers became dominated by the question, "Why, God? Why am I still single?"

One day, she realized that perhaps the reason God had not granted her the gift of marriage was because of her own discontentment. Her quest had become so all-consuming that it actually became an idol. Consider the difference between her attitude and that of Paul when he wrote, "I am not saying this because I am in need, for I have learned to be content whatever the circumstances. I know what it is to be in need, and I know what it is to have plenty. I have learned the secret of being content in any and every situation, whether well fed or hungry, whether living in plenty or in want" (Philippians 4:11–12). How many of us can say that? Instead, whatever the object of our desire might be, we think, *I want it! I must have it! I won't be complete without it!* How often we fall short of Paul's admonition, "Give thanks in all circumstances, for this is God's will for you in Christ Jesus" (1 Thessalonians 5:18).

Over time, this woman began to realize the error of her thinking. She began to change her prayer. She began to pray that God would give her contentment in singleness, *even if she never married.* Fully acknowledging her own personal desire to be married, she nonetheless submitted her desire to God's will. God honored her change of attitude, and a short time later, He did bring a husband into her life.

Don't be deceived into thinking you must find someone to be complete. As a believer in Christ, you are already complete in Him. "And in Him you have been made complete, and He is the head over all rule and authority" (Colossians 2:10 NASB).

Where Are You Finding Fulfillment?

The second most common frustration I hear from single Christians is, "Marriage is the only way to relational fulfillment. If I'm single, I will never have fulfilling relationships." Like the woman described above, some people desire marriage so much that they focus all their time, energy, and attention on finding "the one." They jump from one romantic relationship to the next, searching for true love. As they do, they miss out on many quality nonromantic relationships that they could be enjoying here and now.

It doesn't matter if we are married or single. We need deep, intimate friendships. God created a need in us for companionship. He created us as social beings with the need for fellowship with other people. But it is also true that *He* wants to be our friend. In fact, He is the best friend anyone could ever have. God has never created—nor will ever create—a need in our lives that He cannot fulfill. Throughout the Bible, you will find examples of many individuals who had fulfilling relationships, including the apostle Paul. In fact, the greatest example of a single person with fulfilling relationships is Jesus Christ. I don't really think of Jesus as a single guy, but He was. He was human, and He had the same need for companionship as we do. If you look in the Bible, you will see how Jesus created intimate relationships and developed close, personal bonds of true friendship.

Do you have close friendships? Do you know people to whom you can go and share the intimate details of your life? Do you know people who will pray with and for you? Do you have people in your life who will love you, no matter what? We all need these types of friendships. But where does it start? How does it happen?

The starting place is the number one relationship in your life: with Jesus Christ. Develop your relationship with Him just as He developed His relationship with the Father. Then grow in that relationship. To do this, you must spend time with Jesus. You must talk with Him. You have to share with Him what is on your heart and mind. The way you do this is through prayer, Bible studies, participating in a local church body, and spending personal time with Him. This is not a substitute for being married. It is a prerequisite.

Many people go into marriage thinking that their spouse will fulfill all their needs. Then they marry someone who is flawed and imperfect (someone with a sinful nature like their own), and they are disappointed when their mate falls short of expectations. This leads to marital problems, long-term counseling, and even divorce.

The truth is, *you cannot have a truly fulfilling marriage unless you have a fulfilling relationship with Jesus Christ first!* No human being can fulfill all of your needs—no one. If you are looking for that to happen, you are setting yourself and your future mate up for failure. Only when Jesus Christ is your rock, and in Him you find your complete fulfillment and self-worth, will you be able to weather the storms that come with spending a lifetime with another human being.

So, how is your relationship with God? Is it possible that you have never trusted Jesus Christ as your Lord and Savior? If you have not, or if you are unsure, I strongly urge you to accept your "free gift" at the end of this book.

Finding True Contentment

I don't know where you are with your single life or how much frustration you have experienced with dating. However, I believe that if you can grasp the truth about Jesus Christ, then you will find contentment and fulfillment in being single. As you do, you will find some truly great advantages to being single that outweigh any frustrations you are experiencing today.

Name one! you might say. Okay, I'll sum them up in a single word—freedom! As a single person, we have the freedom to live a simpler life. We have the freedom to set our own schedules. We have the freedom to determine our own priorities. We don't have to deal with the sacrifices and responsibilities that accompany a marriage and family. You may say, "But I want these responsibilities!" It is true, they can offer great joy. At the same time, they are with you every moment of the day, every day of the year. You can't take time off from being a wife or a husband. You can't take a break from being a mother or a father. Once you take on these responsibilities, they are yours for life, with no breaks in-between.

In *Sacred Marriage: What If God Designed Marriage to Make Us Holy More Than to Make Us Happy?*, Gary Thomas writes that the pressures of marriage act as God's refining fire to strip away our selfishness and change and mold our priorities so that serving our own wants and needs drops to the bottom of the list. Only then can we find true fulfillment. "If you want to serve Jesus, stay single," he writes. "If you want to be like Jesus, get married."[1]

As a single person, treasure the freedom you have to serve God with no encumbrances. This is truly a priceless gift. If God does grant us marriage? That is just a bonus.

---

[1] Gary Thomas, *Sacred Marriage* (Grand Rapids: Zondervan Publishing, 2000), p. 21.

CHAPTER TWO

What Are Your Desires?

Delight yourself in the Lord and he will
give you the desires of your heart.

PSALM 37:4

P salm 37:4 is a favorite verse for many Christians, especially those who are looking for a mate. After all, it tells us that if we delight ourselves in the Lord, He will give us what we want, right?

While Psalm 37 does say that the Lord will give us the "desires of our hearts," Jeremiah 17:9 also tells us, "The heart is deceitful above all things and beyond cure. Who can understand it?" On one hand, God promises to give us what we want. On the other hand, our hearts are deceitful. Often, what we want is not good for us. God isn't going to give us something that isn't good for us. How do we reconcile the two verses? Another way to read Psalm 37:4 is, "If I delight in the Lord, He will give me the desires of my heart. However, He is the one who created me, and when He created me, He created pure desires within me—desires that align with His. Therefore, since He knows my desires better than I do, He will fulfill those desires as He sees fit."

See the great irony here? Although Psalm 37 tells us that if we delight in the Lord, He will give us the desires of our hearts; the more we seek the Lord, the more our desires look like His desires. Another Scripture that sheds more light on this is Isaiah 55:11: "So is my word that goes out from my mouth: It will not return to me empty, but will accomplish what I desire and achieve the purpose for which I sent it."

In this passage, the word *desire* tells us something interesting. When we hear God's Word on a matter, it causes us to become aware of the desires He planted within us from the foundation of the world. Therefore, one of the main reasons God speaks is for us to become cognizant of His will, not our own. Once we know His will, and once we seek for it to be fulfilled in our lives, He creates a desire within us that is incredible!

One of these desires is for intimate relationships, marriage, and children. In fact, a friend once pointed out that God's first commandment had to do with these very things. "So God created man in his own image, in the image of God he created him; male and female he created them. God blessed them and said to them, 'Be fruitful and increase in number; fill the earth and subdue it'" (Genesis 1:27–28).

The desires we feel for love, intimacy, and a physical relationship are part of our wiring. God's Word on this has definitely *not* returned to Him void. (There are, after all, more than six billion of us alive today!)

However, it is also true that not all desires are good. Some desires can be very dangerous. We find one story about selfish desire in the earliest part of Genesis. Satan tempted Eve to eat the forbidden fruit, saying, "'For God knows that when you eat of it your eyes will be opened, and you will be like God, knowing good and evil.' When the woman saw that the fruit of the tree was good for food and pleasing to the eye, and also desirable for gaining wisdom, she took some and ate it. She also gave some to her husband, who was with her, and he ate it" (Genesis 3:5–6).

What a sight! Man and woman eating what God had forbidden so they could obtain the selfish desires of their hearts, rather than trusting the perfect will of the God who created them. Remember that, to Adam and Eve, God was a tangible presence. Once He created them, He placed them in an earthly paradise and entrusted it to their care. He even walked with Adam in the cool of the evening. God had said that mankind would be "in our image" and have dominion and lordship over everything that moved upon the earth. What an astounding gift! But that wasn't enough. Satan tempted Adam and Eve to want more. Then he tempted them to fulfill that desire on their own, in their own way, against God's perfect will. We all know the result: expulsion from the Garden of Eden; a life of toil, pain, and physical death; and, outside a saving relationship with Jesus Christ, enmity with God.

Another example of selfish desire is found in Numbers 11, which gives the account of the Israelites' forty years of wandering in the desert. During this journey, they grew tired of eating manna. They wanted something more. They desired meat. Even though God had just freed them from slavery, they longed to return to Egypt, where at least they had food. In essence, they desired things that were not God's best. Even so, God granted their desire by sending quail. The irony is, the Israelites became so consumed with their lust for meat that they got sick from eating it and many died. The place where this occurred is called Kibroth-hattaavah, which literally means "the graves of desire." This name reflects that, when unchecked by a right relationship with Almighty God, our desires can become deadly. They can nullify everything that God has planned for our good. The children of Israel lusted for meat, but what they really needed was to trust the one who created the food and provided for them in due season.

Stalking Our Desires

These biblical perspectives on desire are very important in the context of seeking a mate. Within each of us lives a desire for a relationship and companionship. The question is, as you seek them, whose desire are you following? Your own? Or God's?

Think of how often you may have just wanted to date the best-looking hunk at the coffee shop or the cute gal who works at the bank, even if you know that the apple of your eye is not a Christian. You might know that, as a believer in Christ, you should only date someone who is a Christian, too, but then you begin to think, *I don't care who it is. I just want someone right now. I don't like being alone.* So you get into a relationship with someone who is not at all someone with whom you should share your life. But it doesn't matter because you are living for the moment, for "right now."

Instead of this "right now" attitude, you need to change your thinking to "what's important in the long run." God doesn't want you to settle for whoever will go out with you at the moment. He wants you to have a beautiful, long-lasting relationship with someone who will love you deeply and whom you can love the same way. He wants you to have a relationship with someone who will know you inside and out.

That sounds great, doesn't it? We all want someone who knows us so well that he or she knows our favorite food, our favorite movie, and what makes us laugh or cry. We long to share our lives with someone who has the same godly vision as we do, the same spiritual purpose, so we can travel hand-in-hand and share life's sorrows and joys together. But this person doesn't always come in the package we expect. It is entirely possible that, in seeking what we think we want, we can miss God's perfect plan.

In John 12:25, Jesus says, "The man who loves his life will lose it, while the man who hates his life in this world will keep it for eternal life." In other words, those who hold onto the things that are temporary ("right now") instead of those that will last forever ("the long run") will miss out on eternal blessings because they are living only for what they *think* they need, even if it is not best for them.

Moving Beyond 'Right Now'

I used to live a "right now" life, but one day I stopped and thought, *What am I here for anyway? Is this all there is to life? I work hard every day to achieve my goals, but I feel as though I am wasting my life.* Mentally, I slapped my head. *It is not about me! It is all about*

Him! It was time to start living for the long run and being willing to sacrifice what I wanted now for God's long-term goals.

We also believe we can gratify our own desires. One day, you may see a good-looking person, someone who appeals to your senses. So you introduce yourself. Slowly, you learn more about one another. You really click, and without consulting God, you begin spending time together. As the relationship grows, so does your passion. Your rationale is this: *If I have wants and needs, I need to meet them myself.* So you begin to see how you can satisfy those cravings. Eventually, you start to build an inappropriate intimacy into your relationship. In your heart, you know that this is not the kind of relationship God wants you to have, but you feel you have to satisfy those longings right away. Not too long afterward, a life on track for God is derailed.

This kind of thing results from a shallow and short-sighted view on relationships. Remember God's promises: "And my God will meet all your needs according to his glorious riches in Christ Jesus" (Philippians 4:19). He will meet your needs—and mine. It is not up to us to fulfill our own desires.

The Relationship Idol

Through my relationships, the Lord has revealed that men have been idols in my life. I have been looking to dating relationships, rather than to Him, to fulfill the longing for love burning within me. The reality is, however, no man can love me as deeply and perfectly as I long to be loved. For this kind of love, God must be my all—my everything. He is the one who gave me the desire for love in the beginning; He, and only He, can completely fulfill it.

As long as you try to make someone else your god, you will open yourself to hurt, disappointment, and disillusionment because your expectations can never be met. The reason we want dating relationships, marriage, or other external relationships so much is because God put an innate hunger within us to be

13

lovesick for Him. When we transfer that lovesickness to someone or something else, things are out of balance.

I desire to get married someday, but it is a little scary, too. Did you know that, according to many statistics, more than half of today's marriages end in divorce? According to a study conducted by the George Barna Research Group, the divorce rate among conservative Christians is even higher than that among other faith groups, including atheists and agnostics! As I look around, I see not only from the statistics, but also from my family and friends who have gone through divorce, the kind of pain and heartache that result from a broken marriage. If more than half of marriages end in divorce, clearly, marriage is not something that should be rushed into!

Let me paint a scenario. One day I decide to go shopping in the mall. Before I walk inside, I read a sign on the door that says, "There is at least a 50 percent chance that your car will be stolen while you are shopping here." After reading that, would *you* walk into the mall? Or perhaps I decide to buy a house. The real estate agent shows me one that is in my price range and in an area I really want to live. Then she says, "This house has a number of electrical problems and there is at least a 50 percent chance that it will burn down while you live here." I don't like those odds. Do you? Yet these are the odds we face when making one of the most important decisions in our lives.

So how do we improve the odds? We change our perspective on relationships. We start looking at them the way God does. After all, He is the one who designed them. When I read the Scriptures to see what God has to say about marriage, I learn that He uses it as a reflection of His love for us. The love between a man and woman should reflect the kind of love that Christ has for His Church. It is a kind of love that is so great that He was willing to give up everything, including, and most importantly, His life. He did it so we could understand and experience that love in every fiber of our being.

Consider this passage in Ephesians 5, which God gave us as the basis for all Christian marriages: "Wives, submit to your husbands as to the Lord. For the husband is the head of the wife as Christ is the head of the church, his body, of which he is the Savior. Now as the church submits to Christ, so also wives should submit to their husbands in everything. Husbands, love your wives, just as Christ loved the church and gave himself up for her to make her holy, cleansing her by the washing with water through the word, and to present her to himself as a radiant church, without stain or wrinkle or any other blemish, but holy and blameless. In this same way, husbands ought to love their wives as their own bodies. He who loves his wife loves himself. After all, no one ever hated his own body, but he feeds and cares for it, just as Christ does the church— for we are members of his body" (Ephesians 5:22–30).

Think about this passage—really think about it. Are you ready to love someone this way? Do you trust your cherished one to love *you* this way? If not, this reinforces how important it is to let God's desires rule. If we trust our own instincts, we can easily make mistakes. Just imagine: If Ephesians 5 reflects God's plan for marriage, what would happen if you rushed into marriage with the wrong person?

Even if you are in a relationship with the right person, loving someone to the Ephesians 5 standard is still very challenging. You may think, *I really love this person, but I don't know if I can live out an Ephesians 5 kind of life.* This is one of the reasons we must take marriage so seriously. And yet, God will never call us to do something He will not give us the ability to accomplish. Even if we think it is impossible, He enables us to love this way because He has called us to do it.

How can we develop this kind of love? It is not through attraction or personality. It is based on our character, on trust, and on the core of who we are in Christ. It is our character that determines our priorities, our choices, and the way we are able to love. It is what will give us success in our relationships.

Even though I want to get married someday, I cannot make it happen. I must allow God to transform me as I depend on Him. As I do, I know that He is preparing me for a marriage that will not only be pleasing on my wedding day, but that will be able to weather any storm. That starts with my taking one small step of obedience—to know and trust Him completely first. As I do, I am one step closer to finding "the one."

The Relationship Between Love, Desire, and Motivation

One day, I realized how closely love, desire, and motivation are related. How much I want something—a relationship, job, or the approval of those around me—determines how much effort I put into it. If I don't like a relationship, I don't pursue it. If I don't like my job, I only put in as much time as necessary. If I don't like certain people, I tend to avoid them. This makes it very difficult for us, in our own strength, to love people the way God calls us to. In our natural states, we are only motivated to do and pursue the things we want. It also makes us expect and demand things from those we love that they really aren't responsible for providing.

Although this problem manifests itself in different ways, it really stems from a single source—how much I love and desire God. If I am not complete and fulfilled in my relationship with Him, I will constantly find myself striving for something or someone else to fill the void. I will do this by looking for the "right" person or by demanding things from the person with whom I am currently in a relationship.

Proverbs 19:22 says, "What a man desires is unfailing love." This Scripture is referring to God's love—a pure, constant, untainted, unfailing, and unconditional love. It is a love that only God can provide. This is important because it is only once we have received this love that we can extend it to others.

The Bible says, "We love because he first loved us" (1 John 4:19). This reinforces that we can engage in great relationships and love one another only because God loved us first. It is through His love that we are able to love appropriately. We long to be loved and admired by that special someone, but you should know that God has been loving and admiring you ever since He created you. He is saying, "I know you are not perfect. It doesn't matter what you look like. I'm not interested in how successful you are. I want a relationship with you, and I will always love you."

Because of God's great love, Jesus died on the cross and paid our sin debt in full. On that cross, He poured out His unconditional love. He gave us the opportunity to experience this love. The measure of love—any love—is how much we are willing to sacrifice for another. Jesus went all the way. He showed us that His love is unconditional. It is a love that can truly satisfy the emptiness within us. John 15:13 says, "Greater love has no one than this, that he lay down his life for his friends."

It may take some time to find out what God's will is for a relationship in your life, but God's greatest desire is that you learn to trust Him, love Him, and allow Him to work on your character first. Consider Moses. God planned all along for Moses to lead the Israelites out of Egypt and into the Promised Land, but did He hand Moses this responsibility right away? No! God put Moses through forty years of character building and training before He put His plan into action.

Is the reason you have not yet found a mate because God is somehow still in the process of preparing you? If so, why rush the process? Would you drive across a bridge that was in the middle of construction? Would you move into a house with an unfinished roof? Of course not! So why rush into the second most important decision in your life? You may not know how God is preparing you, but you can be confident that He is. Philippians 1:6 (NKJV) says, "Being confident of this very thing, that He who has begun a good work in you will complete it until the day of Jesus Christ."

God is the one who gives you desires, but it is up to you to ask Him how He wants those desires to be accomplished. If we are to find healthy, satisfying relationships, we should not jump ahead of God. We should not try to take His job or tell Him what to do or when to do it. This means being willing to submit entirely to His will. Romans 12:2 says, "Do not conform any longer to the pattern of this world, but be transformed by the renewing of your mind. Then you will be able to test and approve what God's will is—his good, pleasing and perfect will."

Does this mean that God has someone specific in mind for you? Some people think so, but I believe that's reading too much into it. God has given us His plan for the way people are to relate to one another. He has told us how relationships are designed to work. He has told us how He wants us to grow in our walk with Him, and what kind of people He wants us to be. When we meet someone who fits the bill, we are free to choose whether or not to pursue that relationship. While we are waiting for that special companion, we are to conform our attitudes, goals, and priorities to God's. We will be patient. We won't rush. Then, when we find someone who meets God's standards for being a potential mate, we will know it. Don't get ahead of God. Let Him do the work He wants to do in you so that your relationship radar is operating properly.

Of course, God's will might not be for you to get married at all. This might be hard to accept, but accepting this possibility is part of submitting to God's will. There are no guarantees in life except one: God loves us so much that He has a perfect plan for each of us. That plan was formed before we were even born (Psalm 139), and if we trust Him, He will transform our lives from the inside out. For most people, that includes marriage. For some people, it might not. Either way, we must remember to submit our desires to His so that He can bring us the right one (even if that's Himself) on His terms and in His timing, not ours.

CHAPTER THREE

While You Are Waiting

We live by faith, not by sight.

2 CORINTHIANS 5:7

In our culture, we are accustomed to things running quickly, smoothly, and efficiently, according to our timetables. When things don't go as we expect, we assume that something is wrong.

When I started high school, I expected that during my freshman or sophomore year, I would meet and begin dating the man of my dreams. We would each go to college and continue dating. Shortly after graduation, we would have a nice wedding, find really good jobs, and a few years later, start a family. In my bliss, I would be a stay-at-home mom and continue to live an easy, carefree life. It was my plan, and it sounded great. Apparently, God did not get the memo! Needless to say, my life didn't work out the way I expected, except I did graduate from college.

Although initially I was disappointed that I did not live out this plan, over the years, I have discovered that it is God, not me, who knows the best course for my life. Even though I haven't always gotten what I wanted, I have experienced more joy in following His plan than if I'd followed my own. Proverbs 19:21 says, "Many are the plans in a man's heart, but it is the Lord's purpose that prevails." As a result of being single, I have experienced things I never would have if I'd married right out of college. There have been opportunities I wouldn't have had (including international travel and an incredibly fulfilling overseas ministry) if everything had gone my way.

Perhaps you, too, can relate to what I'm saying. You know what it is like to wait. You don't even have to be single to know that. At some point in our lives, we all have to wait on God for something important.

I know married couples who have been anxiously waiting for a baby for years. I know unemployed people who are urgently waiting for God to open the next door of opportunity. I know people with a history of pain, anger, and suffering who are desperately awaiting emotional or physical healing. The question is not, "Will you have to wait?" It is, "What will you do while you are waiting?" There are a few possibilities. You can worry incessantly. You can attempt to fix everything with your own hands as if to say, "If God can't handle it, I will!" Or, when you feel that you have waited long enough, you may eventually fall into despair. If so, don't give in. Don't give up! Waiting is as important a part of God's design for your life as what you see Him doing right now. God has a purpose in waiting. It is learning how to be patient and to trust Him.

What should you be doing while you wait? The best thing is to rest in God and continually yield to Him. This sounds easy, but if you have ever tried to do it, it is actually very difficult. Oftentimes, it will seem as though God is silent and you are in a long, dark tunnel. If that's how you are feeling today, know that even though you can't see His hand, God is working. Whenever I am in a tunnel like this, I must continually remind myself that God is working out circumstances around me. As you wait, know that He is working out circumstances around you, too. Even so, waiting is hard. We all want to see the evidence of His work immediately. Until then, hearing great stories about how God works out incredible circumstances for others can give us hope while we wait.

One really hot summer, a guy met a girl at a camp where he worked. They connected and hit it off. At the time, he was involved in another relationship, so he didn't pursue her. When summer camp was over, he failed to keep in contact, but the girl was always in the back of his mind. Eventually, his other relationship ended and he began to think about the girl at camp with whom he'd been smitten. But now, he had no idea how to reach her. One day, his phone rang and a telemarketer began her spiel. In a formal voice, she introduced herself and began asking survey questions. When he heard her name, he realized it was the same girl he'd met at camp. The young man revealed who he was. They exchanged information, and you can guess the rest of the story— they are dating and plan to marry!

The moral of this story is: Don't hang up on telemarketers! No, the real moral is that our God is awesome. He brought that couple back together in a way that neither of them could have anticipated. He is so powerful that He can be working, even now, in ways you cannot imagine.

When you don't trust God to prepare the way for you, and instead you attempt to rush things, all too often you'll end up settling for second best. Let's say you meet someone and think, *This person has some wonderful qualities, but there are some other characteristics that I don't like. Because of all the good traits, however, I know if I love this individual enough, he or she will change.* You need to realize that most people don't change just because you hope they will. God's plan is for you to have the very best. He intends for you to walk down that aisle someday, look over at your beloved, and have no doubts. If you wait upon the Lord, you will see God do an incredible job of providing the proper circumstances to bring you to that special someone.

Active Waiting

Waiting may seem passive, but it can be active, too. I am waiting, but I've decided not to sit around and twiddle my thumbs. Instead, I'm actively waiting on God for the person He has planned for me. I do this by praying, *God, will you prepare each of us to be who you want us to be before we meet?* Then I rest and allow God to teach me, grow me, and fulfill in me the works that He has planned for me, knowing that if His plan is marriage, He is using these things to prepare me for an even better marriage than I could have chosen on my own. It may not be the "perfect marriage" as some see it, but it will be perfect for God's purposes.

Waiting is frustrating, but God is continually teaching us to trust and depend on Him to meet our every need. Sometimes, we only learn this lesson when we are waiting. God may be allowing you to wait because He is preparing you for what lies ahead. Or He may be allowing you to wait simply to teach you that He can be trusted.

Sometimes, you may think you are waiting on God, but in reality, He may be waiting on you. Think about the woman in Chapter One. She thought she was waiting on God to bring her a husband, but in time she realized that He had been waiting on *her* to give up her discontentment first. Likewise, the reason you might find yourself waiting may be that God is waiting on you to make a move from disobedience to obedience.

Whenever I find myself waiting, I feel as if I am all alone. At such times, I remind myself that God is at work. He may be busy preparing the way. He may be preparing me. Or He may be waiting on me. There are times when loneliness and emptiness feel like a heavy weight, and even knowing God is working does not change that. Knowing things in our head doesn't always change how we feel.

Depression and anxiety may weigh upon your shoulders. You may feel as if you are in a deep, dark tunnel, and you just want to emerge on the other side. You keep trying to take the next step, hoping to reach the sunshine, but your strength is gone. You think, *I can't go on.* The key to making it just one more day is knowing that at the end of that tunnel is a light of hope. If you can feel its warmth, you will gain strength to keep going. That light is Christ, and its warmth is the love of God that has, as its only goal, what's best for you.

You may be in love with someone. Your wish may be that, one day, that person will figure out that you are everything he or she has ever wanted. You wait patiently for that time to come. What happens if this person marries someone else? Maybe you are praying and tenaciously holding onto the belief that God will heal that loved one who has a terminal illness. What happens if that person dies?

Often, our lives fall apart because the light of hope goes out. This tells me I cannot rely on anything temporary or of my own making. My dependence must be on something that will last forever—something (or someone) I can count on. The only thing (or person) I know that fits this description is God. He is the only one on whom I can depend at all times. He was here before I came to this earth, and He will be here after I'm gone. If my trust is in God, then faith in Him and His will for my life will give me the strength to take one more step.

Isaiah 40:28–31 says, "Do you not know? Have you not heard? The Lord is the everlasting God, the Creator of the ends of the earth. He will not grow tired or weary, and his understanding no one can fathom. He gives strength to the weary and increases the power of the weak. Even youths grow tired and weary, and young men stumble and fall; but those who hope in the Lord will renew their strength. They will soar on wings like eagles; they will run and not grow weary, they will walk and not be faint."

This passage gives me encouragement because I know that if God says it, it is done. Essentially, He says, "If you will hope in Me and base everything that forms your life around Me, then I will give you endurance and strength. In this season of waiting, when you don't understand your circumstances and can't see Me working, I will help you rise above your circumstances. No matter how long it takes, you will be able to accomplish all that I ask of you."

Too often, I know this in my head, but I don't feel it in my heart. When this happens, I have learned that I can't change my heart. I have tried, but it is not something I have the power to do.

But God can—and He is the *only* one who can! All I can change are my actions. The moment I begin to feel hopeless, I have to act on the knowledge that there is hope. Then I must choose to tailor my actions in accordance with God's promises, and He will begin to reshape my heart.

What To Do While Waiting

There are two things you can do while you await reassurance from God. The first thing is to shift the control from your hands to God's.

I love to ski, and the first time I went skiing, I spent some time with a ski instructor. He taught me that whenever I feel as if I am getting out of control, the way to regain control is to shift my weight on the skis. If I'm skiing down a mountain and I see a tree ahead, I obviously want to avoid hitting it. The way to do this is to shift my weight onto my other leg. When I shift my weight, I automatically turn away from the tree. When my other ski touches the ground, I can continue safely down the hill.

The same thing happens in our walk with Christ. There are times when I am headed straight for a tree. I am so consumed with worry, stress, and desperation that I feel as if I'm heading straight for a collision. However, if I'm willing to shift the weight of my concerns, worries, and fears to God, I will miss the obstacle completely. If I place all of my trust in God and let Him be in complete control, He will change my direction, move me back to safety, and restore a sense of hope and joy.

The second thing to do while waiting is to follow God's instructions. On my first day of skiing, I actually made it down a mountain with no struggles. On my next attempt, I decided to ski straight down the run and not shift my weight or make any turns at all. As I pushed off down the hill, I immediately began to feel out of control. I realized I had fallen back into my natural inclinations—the ones the ski instructor had tried to break. I wiped out.

My skis and poles went everywhere. When I got up, I thought to myself, *Okay, Emily, your instructor told you exactly what you needed to do to make it through, so do what he said.* The rest of the way down the mountain, I began to transfer my weight as he had taught me, and I came through with precision. This is what God wants for you!

When you are stressed and waiting, it is too easy to fall into bad habits. Resist! My mother once said, "When you don't know what step to take next, do what God has already told you to do." In other words, be obedient. Shift control to God and stick with His instructions.

CHAPTER FOUR

The Differences May Surprise You

So God created man in his own image, in the image of God
he created him; male and female he created them.

GENESIS 1:27

At the beginning of any new relationship, everything seems to go just right. As time passes, however, you start to see changes. The relationship becomes increasingly difficult. You start bickering. You are not as quick to understand and forgive. You start building a wall between you, brick by brick. Before you know it, you are both thinking, *Maybe this person isn't as right for me as I once thought,* and you are on your way to a breakup or divorce.

In part, these struggles occur because men and women are so different. We think differently, we respond differently, and we have different needs and expectations. The healthy way to deal with these conflicts is to understand and relate to one another in the unique ways God created us. Instead, we think the best way to "fix" the relationship is to change our mates so that they think and act like us. No wonder men and women have been in conflict since the beginning!

Most men and women are clueless when it pertains to the opposite sex. Men do not fully perceive the needs and desires of women. Women do not fully comprehend the needs and desires of men. That's why books like *The Five Love Languages* and *Men Are from Mars and Women Are from Venus* have been so successful. Men and women cannot satisfy one another's needs if they do not understand what those needs are. This becomes an even bigger challenge when we realize that men and women often speak two entirely different "languages." Before we can start a dialog, we have to learn the translation!

Two Different Languages

Another book about the differences between men and women is *You Just Don't Understand* by linguist Deborah Tannen, Ph.D. In its pages, Tannen discusses how something as simple as the words "I'm sorry" can lead to worlds of misunderstanding. When a woman says she's sorry, she often means, "I feel badly that…" When a man says he's sorry, he sees it as an apology. Thus, something as simple as "I'm sorry that you tripped over those clothes in the hallway" can be interpreted in two different ways. When a woman says it, she means, "I feel badly that you twisted your ankle." What a man hears, however, is often completely different. He hears, "I'm responsible for your injury because I left the clothes in the way." Needless to say, a seemingly innocent comment can result in a big fight.

These issues arise in nonverbal communication, too. Take what happens if a man comes home and immediately begins reading the newspaper rather than asking about his wife's day. Tannen argues that a woman's world is based on connectivity and socialization. To her, the moment he flips up those pages, he's saying, "I'm shutting you out." Because a man's world is based on competition—one-upmanship—when he immediately settles in with his newspaper, it can be like saying, "I can let my hair down and relax around you." It can actually be a sign of intimacy.

Of course, these are merely precipitating factors. It is how these challenges are handled that can either make them a nonissue or initiate conflict. In his highly successful book *Love and Respect: The Love She Most Desires, the Respect He Desperately Needs*, Dr. Emerson Eggerichs looks at one of the most damaging communication cycles caused by such differences—a cycle that, if not addressed, can destroy even the strongest marriages. It is what he calls "The Crazy Cycle." Eggerichs argues that, at a very fundamental level, women need to be loved, while men need to be respected. These are two entirely different worldviews that, unless understood and accommodated, can result in escalating cycles of frustration and misunderstanding.

For example, when a woman feels hurt or unloved (say, when her husband comes home and reads the newspaper instead of asking her about her day), she tends to complain and criticize. This makes her husband feel disrespected. When a man feels disrespected, he tends to clam up and withdraw. This makes his wife feel unloved, so to regain that love, she fires up the communication machine—she nags, complains, and criticizes. This makes her husband feel even more disrespected, so he shuts down all the more. This makes her feel even more unloved, which makes her escalate the nagging, complaining, and criticizing, which makes him… Well, you get the picture. These two entirely different communication styles act in conflict, with devastating results.

The important point is that, *initially,* neither the man nor the woman is necessarily wrong. God designed men to need respect and women to need love. But without an understanding of how the other might be reacting to what we say or do, and without the tools to respond appropriately, we end up making decisions that only fuel the conflict. Women must learn to anticipate and accommodate how men think (*How will my boyfriend/husband react to what I'm saying? Will he feel respected or disrespected?*). Men must learn to anticipate and accommodate how women think (*If I do this, will my girlfriend/wife feel loved or unloved?*). This is a fundamental shift that can take a long time to learn. Yet, such differences are part of God's grand design.

Another example of fundamental differences between men and women is how they process information. Bill and Pam Farrel expound on these differences in their book *Love to Love You.*

When it comes to the way men and women think, we are radically different. We like to say that men are like waffles and women are like spaghetti. Let's take a look at men first. Men compartmentalize life, focusing on one thing at a time. It is like this—when you look at a waffle, you see lots of individual boxes with walls in between them. Men deal with life as if their brains contained a waffle. They take one issue and put it in a box, then take the next issue and place it in another separate box. If we could see a man's thoughts, they would look just like a waffle, with each little box holding an individual area of life. This causes men to do only one thing at a time. When men are at work, they are at work. When men are doing yardwork, they are doing yardwork. When men are fishing, they are fishing. And when your loved one is thinking about being intimate with you, that's all he's thinking about!

Women, on the other hand, experience life more like a plate of spaghetti. If you look at a plate of spaghetti, you immediately notice that everything touches everything else. That is how women think—they connect every issue. Women have this incredible ability to deal with everything simultaneously. Since it is impossible to fix everything and have it all under control, women fit everything in life together emotionally, feeling something about each issue in their lives. Women may feel happy emotions like sentimentality, joy, and enthusiasm, or they may feel sad emotions like depression or frustration. But the key is to experience some emotion. Once women have emotionally connected with each issue in their lives, they will relax and begin to enjoy the world around them. Women are terrific at combining things. In the same half hour, they can call a friend, plan a special dinner, run a business meeting, write a Christmas card, check in with the kids, and not miss a beat![2]

Think about the last argument you witnessed (or participated in) between a man and a woman. You'll quickly see how these differ-

---

[2] Bill Farrel and Pam Farrel, *Love to Love You* (Eugene, Ore: Harvest House Publishers, 1997), pp. 34–35.

ences can create complications. Say a wife is upset by how her husband acts around her parents. She brings up the issue and he downplays it as being an isolated incident. Therefore, to make her point, she begins to bring up every incident of this same offense, going back ten years. She also ties his behavior in to how he treats members of *his* family. The goal is simply to get him to recognize the importance of the problem, but because he doesn't make the same spaghetti-like connections, he sees these as unrelated personal attacks. In the end, she works against herself. Instead of helping him to understand, she's offended him and made him angry.

How Differences Play Out

Of course, we can't discuss the differences between men and women without talking about getting to the point. Men are goal-oriented, so they like to get to the point right away. This can be a real frustration for many women, who find it difficult to be confrontational for fear of rejection. Often, women just need a shoulder to lean on. They want someone to listen. If they need advice, they will say so. Men, in their well-meaning way, often respond by giving the very thing women don't want—advice—which just upsets and frustrates them. So guys, unless the woman in your life *asks* for your advice, the best thing you can do is take your concerns to God in prayer and allow Him to be the advice-giver.

On the flip side, women are often not as direct in expressing themselves as men are. In a woman's world, not every conversation has to have a goal. It is about the art of communicating, talking, and revealing thoughts and feelings. It is *feeling* those feelings and listening that matters most. In other words, sometimes, the conversation itself is the point. Men, women will judge how much you care by how attentively you listen. Likewise, women, remember that, when dealing with men, they often just want to reach the goal. If your boyfriend is telling you about a problem, ask questions later if you need to, but initially, make it your priority to let him get to his point.

A Look at Romance

Another area of difference between men and women is romance. While many people think of women as being the romantic ones, I would argue that the man is responsible for romance in his marriage. After all, God has given men the responsibility for leadership in the home. This is a leadership that leads by example (Ephesians 5:22–24; Matthew 20:24–26). By implication, that includes romance!

Men, if you don't have romance in you, you had better develop some. Loving your wife is a biblical command, and for a woman, that includes romance. There is not one woman out there who does not desire to be treated with tenderness, love, care, and delicateness by her man. This isn't just women being "mushy" or "overly soft." These desires were placed within women by God as an illustration of His love for us. After all, God is romantic (just look at the Song of Solomon!). He has much more than a legalistic relationship with us. He loves us deeply with an everlasting love.

The challenge for both men and women is that romance isn't something that just "happens," especially as a marriage progresses. Unless you are jet-setters without the normal responsibilities of everyday life, inevitably, married people find that their lives transition from that "high" of courtship to the daily grind. No matter how exciting life was when you were single, you'll wake up one day and find that your big excitement is debating whether to watch chick flicks or action movies on a Friday night. This is normal, and in order to counteract it, you must make plans (such as planning a "date night" every week) to keep the romance and intimacy alive.

Another area we need to review is the differences in feelings. When a man gets hurt, he becomes frustrated and angry. When a woman gets hurt, she feels anxious or dejected. Women have very fragile emotions, and unfortunately, men tend to downplay them or dismiss them as overreactions. This is why God commands, "Husbands, in the same way be considerate as you live with your wives, and treat them with respect as the weaker partner and as heirs with you of the gracious gift of life, so that nothing will hinder your prayers" (1 Peter 3:7). Wow! A woman's emotions are so important to God that, if you trample them, your prayer life may become less effective. So be sensitive.

Sometimes, this is easier said than done. This sensitivity is easy to show early on in your relationship, but as time wears on, the emotional baggage that comes with little hurts and offenses can turn that sensitivity into granite. To prevent this from happening, maintain that tenderness to one another's feelings as diligently as polishing your car or keeping track of the latest football scores. Be careful not to allow those "bricks" to pile up and create a wall between you.

This doesn't let women off the hook, of course. As important as it is for men to attend to their mate's feelings by connecting with them when they are hurt or angry, it is just as important for women to give their men time and space when they are frustrated or angry. Even if you feel that your man is in the wrong, just because you desire to tell him so doesn't mean you have to do it in the heat of the moment. Sometimes, picking *when* to speak is as important as choosing what you actually say.

Like It or Lump It

Even after this, do you think you and your potential mate aren't really that different? Let me give some lighter examples that I regularly see in my counseling sessions:

When men have friendships, how do they get close? They insult each other. They are like two dogs trying to get the other one by the throat. On a Monday morning, one man might greet his close friend by saying, "Hey dude! Your football team is so lame! They couldn't find the end zone if you took 20 yards off the field!" When was the last time you heard two girls doing the same? "Hey, girl, what happened to your makeup? Did you put it on in the dark this morning?" Instead, how do women get close? They hug and encourage each other. Rather than being competitive, they show empathy and emotional support.

What do men usually do when they are under pressure? The majority just want to get away from the source of the stress. They go hang out with the guys, spend time alone, play golf, or watch sports. Women do not understand this. They feel a need to share their problems when they are stressed. Consequently, they feel rejected when men don't do the same. Although women may want their men to come to them with their problems, the best thing they can actually do is respect their man's time away from them. Women, if you feel hurt and let down, take the concern to God and allow Him to heal the hurt you are experiencing.

Expectations about the relationship differ too. A man marries a woman hoping that she won't change, but she does. A woman marries a man hoping that he will change, but he doesn't.

Differences Don't Disappear

There are far more differences between men and women than I can talk about here. The important thing is simply to recognize that these differences exist. Like it or not, God wired us differently. When you are dating, these differences seem minimal. Love conquers all, right? Unfortunately, this is not what plays out in real life. The longer you are married, the clearer these differences become.

Once we understand and accept the fact that men and women are different, however, we can enjoy one another and have a deeper, closer, and more understanding relationship. We can have confidence in the certainty that these differences were planned by God based on His infinite wisdom. Think about it this way: God's goal is not to make you comfortable, but to conform you to the image of His Son (Romans 8:29). It is only once you make the commitment to share the rest of your life with someone who has fundamentally different needs, personality traits, and goals that you begin to understand your own inherent selfishness and inflexibility. If you were to marry someone just like you, those weaknesses would never be exposed. So what better way for God to accomplish His goal than to pair two very different people in a lifetime commitment?

That's why it is critical to be aware that these differences go beyond superficial personality and preferences. They are woven into the very fabric of how men and women think and respond to one another. Rather than needing to be changed, differences were placed there by God for a purpose. Instead of ignoring them, seek to understand and accommodate them.

Before you get married, study up!

CHAPTER FIVE

Preparing on the Inside

Even so faith, if it has no works, is dead, being by itself.

JAMES 2:17 NASB

I went out with my first real boyfriend, Matt, when I was in the third grade. Matt and I had a very simple relationship. We didn't have any problems with communication because we didn't communicate. One day, he sent me a note in class that said, "Will you go out with me?" The note I sent back said, "Yes."

He hung out a bit at school with me, but not that much. After two months, he called me on the phone for the first time. A few months later, he started going out with one of my friends. He never actually broke up with me, so technically, we are still going together to this day. Matt and I didn't have to struggle with the physical part of our relationship. We held hands one time, and that was all. I remember it clearly. We were performing a children's musical at school. We *all* had to hold hands, and Matt just happened to be standing next to me. Matt had the two qualities that I was most looking for in a guy. First, he was cute (all of my friends said so). Second, he was generous. He always let me cut in front of him in line on the playground. He was the man of my dreams.

If you are like me, as time has passed and you have grown wiser, relationships have become more complicated. Notably, you grapple with communication. You may also wrestle with physical intimacy (no pun intended).

Maybe you have written a list of things you are looking for in a person. If this list isn't written down, I'm sure you have one etched in your mind. As time goes forward, you may find your list growing longer and much more complicated. When you meet someone, you scroll down in your head to see how many of your criteria this person meets. If he or she meets at least one or two, you might ask for a date. We all have those lists.

The list of things I'm looking for in another person is long. As I've matured, however, I have realized that a relationship is not about who is most attractive to me. It is not about the person who can best provide for me or whom I enjoy hanging out with the most. It is about finding someone with whom I can have a long-lasting relationship, and in that relationship, reflect to the world how Christ loves us and the Church. When I look at relationships that way, it sure narrows my list.

Another irony is that, although we have lists, we very seldom make lists of things in ourselves that we need to improve to make us more desirable to someone else. We should know what we're looking for in the other person, but it is more important to look at ourselves and strive to become the kind of person God wants us to be. The more time you spend preparing yourself, the less time you will spend being dissatisfied that you have not yet found that special someone.

Find Your Confidence

So how do you prepare yourself? First, you must be confident. When I say confidence, I am not talking about having the biggest ego or liking yourself perfectly. Being confident means being complete and filled with the Holy Spirit. It means not being a person who is desperately looking for someone else to fill your void. You don't want to be someone who is so desperate for love and attention that you will cling to the first person you meet.

Have you ever talked with someone who has low self-esteem? These people are constantly needing affirmation, desperately wanting to feel loved and expecting their mates to meet needs that only God can fulfill. Although their loved ones may care about them, meeting their mate's every need is not their job. Nor could they do it, even if they wanted to. God did not intend for people to do that for each other. The only person who can love you perfectly and meet all of your needs is Jesus Christ. If you—or I, or anyone else—expect that from another person, we are asking for something that cannot be done. We will never feel completely loved, and we will drain the other person.

Until you allow God's love to permeate you, you cannot fully love someone else. You must be content with who you are in Christ, and you must recognize that you are a unique, gifted person created by God. Only then can you give love freely without demanding love back. You must be someone who is Christ-confident. You must be looking for someone with the same kind of Christ-confidence, too.

Become a Servant

The next thing you will want to do is become a servant. Be a person who displays in every action, every word, and every decision an attitude of humility. Paul makes this clear in Philippians 2:5–8: "Your attitude should be the same as that of Christ Jesus: Who, being in very nature God, did not consider equality with God something to be grasped, but made himself nothing, taking the very nature of a servant, being made in human likeness. And being found in appearance as a man, he humbled himself and became obedient to death—even death on a cross!"

If you want your relationship to reflect Christ's love for the Church, you must be committed to being a servant. This means being humble. Christ loved us so much that He took upon Himself the limitations of a man, and He died for us. Now that is true love! What does that look like in a relationship? I can tell you what it doesn't look like. It doesn't look like trying to force your way, always trying to get in the last word, or always trying to prove that you are right. It doesn't matter if you are right. Your goal shouldn't be to *prove* that you are right.

Become someone who is flexible, patient, and understanding. Practice serving others now, in your conversations, friendships, and relationships. Learn to allow others to have their way. Let them do what they want. This is how you learn to be a servant. While you are doing so, look for someone else who is a servant, too—someone who is courteous, kind, considerate, and helpful; someone who puts the needs of others before their own.

Be Committed

The third thing is the need to be committed. In the Bible, we find a great example of this: "The Lord is faithful to all his promises and loving toward all he has made" (Psalm 145:13). In Himself, God has given us the perfect example of commitment. Someone who is committed is willing to keep trying when times get tough rather than giving up and walking away. Not only do you—yourself—need to work through the hard times, but you want to marry someone who is willing to work just as hard as you will.

When I was young, I mistakenly thought if I ever got into an argument with someone I was dating, we were incompatible. Obviously, if he couldn't see things my way, then he wasn't right for me. The man of my dreams would always agree with me. I have learned a lot since then. Now I realize that, while in a relationship, I have to be willing to go through the hard times. If there is a fight or disagreement, I need to stick with the person and work through it. That might mean not getting my own way.

Practice commitment in relationships now, whether in dating relationships, friendships, family relationships, or work relationships. For example, when things get rough at my job, if I don't get along with my co-workers, if I don't reach all my goals, that doesn't mean I quit and stomp out of the office. It simply means I should continue moving forward in my present position. When I have a disagreement with a friend, that doesn't mean I turn my back on her and hang out with someone else. We work through it so we can have a deeper and stronger relationship.

As I observe the relationships around me, I see challenges everywhere. Out of all of those relationships, I have never seen one that didn't experience some rough times. I know of some incredible marriages between people who have completely committed to one another, but I have never seen a marriage that has always been easy. Remember, you have committed to that person for a lifetime. You can't just walk out and start over as you can with a friendship or a job. If you don't learn to resolve conflicts in a healthy way, hurt and resentment will build up very quickly. Then it has a lifetime to sit there. Unresolved conflict will ruin a marriage more quickly than you can imagine.

Look for Similar Priorities

The fourth thing you need is to have similar priorities. That doesn't mean you must agree with everything the other person does, but it does mean that you should have comparable values and priorities. After all, you will be spending a lot of time together.

In Matthew 6:19-21, Jesus says, "Do not store up for yourselves treasures on earth, where moth and rust destroy, and where thieves break in and steal. But store up for yourselves treasures in heaven, where moth and rust do not destroy, and where thieves do not break in and steal. For where your treasure is, there your heart will be also." Some day, I hope to find someone who puts his treasure in the same places I do. That means while I'm single, I need to get my priorities straight. Where do I commit my time? My money? My energy? Do I invest in things that will rust and be destroyed or eaten away? Or do I invest in things that will last forever?

Someone once said if you want to know to whom you are committed, look at your calendar and your checkbook. Your commitments to God (or lack thereof) will be evident. Our number one priority should be our relationship with Jesus Christ. Our goal should be to glorify Him in everything we do, whether we are at work, at the grocery store, or hanging out with friends.

Be a Communicator

The fifth area on which you need to work is becoming a better communicator. Communication is extremely important, and a relationship cannot exist without it. This doesn't mean we need to be nonstop talkers. Talking takes only one person, but communication takes two. You need to find someone with whom you can be open and honest, and vice versa. You need to know that you can say what is on your mind and know you can trust the other person to keep it confidential. There will also be seasons of laughter and tears, and you need to find someone whom you can trust, so you can be yourself during these times.

The Most Important Commitment

Finally, and most importantly, you need to be committed to God. If you cannot commit yourself to God, the one who loves you perfectly and will never fail you, how will you be able to commit to another person who will let you down routinely? If you are committed to God, you will reflect His character in your everyday actions. It will be evident by the way you live your life, even in the very words you choose. You *must* find someone who is dedicated to the Lord. In 2 Corinthians 6:14, Paul says, "Do not be yoked together with unbelievers." When I weigh whether to spend time with a person, I need to know whether he will encourage and help me grow in the most important relationship in my life—with Jesus Christ.

You must be the kind of person spiritually that you are seeking to find. If you want someone who is committed to prayer and reading the Bible, you must be committed to prayer and reading the Bible, too.

Here is a picture of what a relationship looks like when two individuals are pursuing God and putting Him first in their lives:

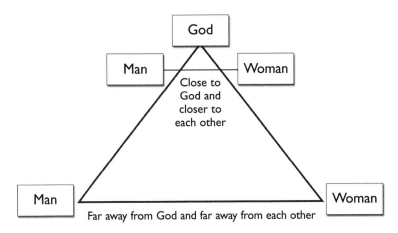

If both you and your loved one are remote from God, you will be distant from each other, too. If only one of you is moving closer to God, your relationship will be out of balance and you will grow more distant over time. But when two people grow closer to God individually, they will grow closer to each other because any man or woman fully committed to the Lord has all of the tools needed to have a successful relationship. This doesn't mean that a relationship will automatically be smooth (chances are, it won't), but you will be in the strongest position to make a good choice in your future mate. So allow God to work in each of you as you work out the rough edges and commit to one another.

CHAPTER SIX

Are You Choosing or Settling?

*But seek first his kingdom and his righteousness,
and all these things will be given to you as well.*

MATTHEW 6:33

Over the past few years, I have consulted with many singles to glean exactly what they are looking for in a mate. I have received a wide variety of responses. I remember one saying, "I don't know," then shrugging and staring at the wall behind me. After a few moments, she came up with an answer: "Blue eyes!"

For the most part, single adults are not able to articulate what they are looking for in the person they are hoping to spend the rest of their lives with. No wonder the divorce rate is so high! If you don't know what you are looking for, how will you ever know when you have found it? Many singles think they'll "know it when they see it," but too often, this results in an emotion-driven experience that leads us astray. Next to your relationship with Jesus Christ, choosing a mate is the most important decision you'll ever make. You ought to be clearer than that!

Even though the word "dating" is not used in the Bible, the principles for successful courtship are given to us in our guidelines for all interpersonal relationships. The Bible says that, after creating man, God declared, "It is not good for the man to be alone" (Genesis 2:18). Then He created woman as a suitable helper for him. At that moment, romance, marriage, and commitment became the very fabric of society.

A dating relationship is the period of time during which two people determine whether they are right for each other. This vital relationship can potentially lead to marriage. Even if it does not, it is a time of valuable learning.

Dating is a terrific opportunity to experience interpersonal growth. It is the occasion to learn the "language" of the opposite sex, to develop a better understanding of human needs, and to learn how to relate to someone on a deep, intimate level. The more people you spend emotionally intimate time with, the clearer picture you'll get of the kind of person with whom you want to spend the rest of your life. When you finally do commit, it will be evident how important it is to get it right the first time.

Before You Make 'The Big One'

Even if you haven't sat down and really thought about what you are looking for, there are some basics you ought to keep in mind. Granted, there are preferences that will be unique to you. Some people are looking for a mate who loves the outdoors. Others are looking for someone who loves the city life. Some might prefer a mate who plays tennis. Others might prefer someone who plays soccer. These preferences will vary from person to person, but if you are a Christian, there is a set of characteristics that ought to apply across the board, to every potential marriage partner, regardless of personal preferences.

1. Commitment to Christ

The person you are interested in should be committed to Christ. You should be able to share the most important relationship in your life with him or her. The Scriptures are very clear: "Do not be yoked together with unbelievers. For what do righteousness and wickedness have in common? Or what fellowship can light have with darkness?" (2 Corinthians 6:14). Here, the apostle Paul is communicating this principle using an agricultural analogy. In ancient times, a pair of oxen were used to pull a plow. In order to pull evenly, a single wooden yoke extended across the backs of the necks of both animals so they could pull in harmony. What do you think happened when the oxen were pulling in opposite directions? How much plowing got done? Not much! Or the ground would be plowed unevenly and would not be useful for planting.

The same concept applies to marriage. If only one spouse is a believer, the two will always be pulling in different directions. Even if you think you both have the same goals and priorities, you'll quickly discover how untrue this really is. The apostle James wrote that those who walk in the ways of the world make themselves the enemies of God (James 4:1–4). Those are strong words. The context is referring to believers who walk in their old ways rather than in the Spirit of God, but if a believer's friendship with the world makes him an enemy of God, imagine the condition of someone who has not surrendered his life to Jesus Christ! Do you want to be married to an enemy of God? Do you think that God's child and God's enemy can live together in harmony? Do you think a Christian can be fully used by God, free to do His will, when "yoked" to someone whose nature is at enmity with theirs? Any Christian who is considering marrying an unbeliever would do well to carefully consider these two passages.

Keep in mind, too, that just claiming to be a Christian doesn't make you one. I know a woman who was once deeply in love with a man who was not a believer. At the time they met, she had never really committed her life to Christ, but during the course of their relationship, she fully surrendered to Him. Soon, the truth of the Scriptures caused her to break off the relationship. Her boyfriend was stunned. He tried to woo her back by insisting that because he, too, believed in the moral teachings of Jesus, this made him a Christian. It took a lot of strength for her to resist this argument, but she understood that being a Christian isn't what you do. It is a fundamental change in your nature, a supernatural act of God that occurs, not with an intellectual recognition of the wisdom of Jesus' teachings, but at the moment someone asks Jesus, the head of all creation, to forgive their sins and be Lord of their lives. Only then does God make us new creations (2 Corinthians 5:17) and we pass from spiritual death to life. Only two people who have accepted Christ in this way are equally yoked.

Of course, some people will do anything or say anything to be with someone they love. They will claim to become (or already be) Christians. They will even be baptized. For this reason, you cannot rely on a hormone-driven decision in choosing your future mate. If you are dating someone who is not a believer, back off. Even if that person claims to become a believer, watch and see what happens. If this person becomes a true Christ-follower, actively and visibly growing and making Jesus first in his or her life, then you can (and perhaps should) consider dating again.

But even if—and this is a big "if"—the person truly does become a Christ-follower, keep in mind that growing in Christ is much like growing from childhood into adulthood. The writer of Hebrews referred to the spiritually immature as being able to take only baby's milk and the spiritually mature as being able to take solid food (Hebrews 5:12–14). Even if someone becomes a Christian, that person will be at the beginning of his or her spiritual journey. If you have been a believer for some time, there can still be a large differential in your understandings. As you enter marriage together, that difference can present challenges you do not anticipate.

Some people will insist, "I'm not thinking about investing the rest of my life in this relationship," or, "I am just casually dating, so it doesn't matter if this person is a Christian or not." You are not fooling anyone—certainly not God. It doesn't matter if you go out for coffee, to a movie, or anywhere else. Every time you date, no matter how casually, you still end up asking yourself, *Could this be the one?* Do not fall into this trap. Even if you know that a relationship shouldn't lead to marriage, your heart can get in the way.

Her charming smile. His sense of humor. Her caring touch. His twinkling eyes. Before you know it, emotions are running deep and it becomes increasingly difficult to break it off. Not only will you get hurt, but the other person will, too. Jesus was very clear about flirting with sin—any kind of sin. This includes inappropriate relationships. We should cut off our involvement in such things immediately. This principle was so important that He taught on it twice (Matthew 5:30, 18:8).

2. Commitment to Marriage

Before making a decision, you need to know if your loved one is committed to marriage. A marriage without commitment is like a Harley without handlebars. It might look good and sound good, with its hearty *vroom, vroom, vroom*, but without this critical piece of equipment, you cannot steer it.

When you have a relationship lacking commitment, it is like using a rental car compared to driving your own vehicle. When we rent an automobile, we really don't take very good care of it. We don't want any major accidents, of course, but we don't care if a French fry gets smashed into the upholstery, if we spill soda on the floor mat, or if a rock hits the windshield. It's just a rental car. But if it is our own car, we take meticulous care of it, don't we?

I own a late model vehicle, and needless to say, I am concerned about my car. When I first drove my car into a parking lot, I parked as far away from all the other cars as I could. Why? Because I didn't want so much as a door ding on it. Even now, when my friends get into my car with food or drink, I think, *Don't eat in here! Watch that drink!* After all, I have invested something in it. This holds true for relationships, too. They mean so much more when you have something invested in them.

This goes beyond commitment to a person and includes commitment to the concept of marriage itself. There often comes a point in marriages in which the couples' commitment to the very foundational principles of marriage will be tested. I know of one couple whose premarital counselor shocked them by saying, "There will come a point in your marriage when you will be lying in bed, look over at your spouse, and a cold shudder will run down your spine. You will think, 'Why on earth did I marry this person?' It is not a matter of 'if.' It is a matter of 'when.'"

Ironically, this is a very normal part of marriage. The challenges and struggles of life can take a tremendous toll. You may think you are so deeply in love that nothing could shake your emotions, but after years of the daily grind—getting up, going to work, dealing with stress at home and your place of work, paying bills, disciplining children—it is easy to end up in a situation you never anticipated. What happens when you two enter a long period of emptiness? Or if troubles in your marriage lead to years of strife? What if, through a prolonged illness, depression, or loss, one of you undergoes a personality change?

A commitment, not just to a person, but to the fundamental tenets of marriage, creates a level of endurance that enables you to work through extended hardship. When you are in your twenties or thirties, it is hard to imagine long "wilderness" periods that can last, not just weeks or months, but years—even decades. It happens more often than singles realize. Especially in Christian circles, people put on a happy face and pretend that everything is fine. But the reality is, the rates of divorce among Christian couples are the same (or even higher) as those among unbelievers.

3. Character

The third issue I want to address is character, because in the long run, it is character that really counts.

Gals, when you are dating a new guy, the first thing your girlfriends will ask is, "What does he do?" Guys, when you are dating a new girl, the first inquiry that your buddies will make is, "What does she look like?" When this happens, consider the wisdom recounted in 1 Samuel 16:7: "The Lord does not look at the things man looks at. Man looks at the outward appearance, but the Lord looks at the heart."

How do you see into the heart of another individual? How do you discern someone's character or moral strength? During the early period, one way to do this is to interview the one you are dating. Do the tough work *before* you allow the bells of matrimony to ring. Sit down and ask each other questions like these:

1. What would your ex-boyfriends or ex-girlfriends say your weakest character flaws are and why?
2. What do you hope to improve about yourself over the next five years?
3. How intimate is your relationship with God?
4. How often do you pray and read the Bible?
5. What are your goals?
6. What is most important to you in a relationship?

Next, interview yourself. Ask questions such as: Do I want to spend the rest of my life with this person, even if he or she never changes? Do I want children who act in the same manner as this person? A lot of us marry the potential of a person and not the reality. We will often tell ourselves things like, "I want to marry this person because of what he or she can accomplish." Or, "Look what they can be under the right circumstances!" Instead, ask yourself, "Do I want to become more like this person? Does this person allow Christ to shine through him or her?" If this person is a worthwhile candidate for a date (let alone marriage!), the answers to these questions should be "yes."

Another thing that is extremely helpful in discerning another person's character is playing games together. It doesn't matter what those games are. They could be putt-putt, dominoes, tennis, cards, or pool—it doesn't matter. Just play. Why? Because competitive situations bring out a person's character.

Another way to reveal someone's character is to see how he (or she) treats parents and siblings. It is easy to treat someone well when a relationship is fresh. It is over time that challenges take their toll. How your potential spouse treats his or her family members reveals a lot about how he or she handles long-term conflict. Does he allow bitterness and resentment to build up? Does she show care and concern, even if there are differences of opinion over long periods of time? If your future spouse is unforgiving toward a parent, chances are that he or she will be unforgiving toward you, too.

Character is crucial. Ultimately, it determines how this person will treat himself or herself, how this person will act toward others (especially you), and how he or she will treat future children. Good family relationships don't guarantee good marital relationships, of course, but poor family dynamics can pretty much guarantee poor marital relationships. There is an old saying that, if you want to know how a man will treat his wife, look at how he treats his mother. There is a lot of truth to that—for both men and women.

4. Acceptance and Contentment

Be sure this person accepts you just the way you are. I can't stress enough that he or she needs to be content with you, no matter what. This doesn't mean that this person overlooks when you act in sinful ways. It means that he or she understands and accepts what makes you "you," with the preferences, quirks, and personality traits with which God designed you.

I know a woman who once dated a man whom she loved deeply but who always seemed to want her to be someone else. He said that he loved her, but he was always dissatisfied. When they went bicycling, he wanted her to cycle faster and harder, like he did. When they went on picnics, he got angry if she didn't pack the basket exactly as he would have. When she experienced problems at work, he insisted that she handle them his way. He said he loved her for *her*, but more and more, it seemed to her that what he really wanted was someone who thought and acted exactly like he did. Ultimately, she realized that she could never live up to his expectations. While it was an enormously painful decision, she ended the relationship.

In addition to looking for someone who accepts you for "you," look for someone who is content in the broader areas of life. Beware of the individual who says, "I need this. I must have that." If someone feels that he or she must drive this particular model car, make a specific amount of money, or live in a certain kind of house, look for the nearest exit and *run*. God doesn't intend for things to be more important than people. In Luke 12:15, Jesus says, "'Watch out! Be on your guard against all kinds of greed; a man's life does not consist in the abundance of his possessions.'" We might not think of this as greed (we may see it as an issue of priorities), but it is. Not only this, but all aspects of our lives are in God's hands, including possessions. God will give us what we need, not always what we want or demand. It is always His will we are to seek, not our own (James 4:13–15).

Beware of anyone who sees you as filling a need or part of a specific life plan. You cannot meet anyone else's every need—only God can do that. Even the best life plans get derailed. It is better to know that this person is going to love and value you for who you are, not for what you do, what you look like, or the role you may play. You want someone who will see you as the gift from God that you are, not someone to be molded or changed, or who can help him or her accomplish personal goals.

5. Best Friends for Life

The last question you should ask is, "Is the person I intend to marry my best friend?" He (or she) should be. Friendship should be extremely important in a dating relationship. Unfortunately, this role is often sidetracked by physical appearance. More important is that you share a common faith in Christ, similar life goals, and mutual interests, such as politics, sports, music, art, or professional pursuits. Be assured, if you don't take the time necessary to build a friendship, you will have much pain down the road. Remember 1 Samuel 16:7: "Man looks at the outward appearance, but the Lord looks at the heart." The focus of your friendship should be on getting to know the other person's heart, not on creating premature intimacy and emotional dependence.

In the end, more important than any of these is a strong personal relationship with Jesus Christ. This should be the foundation of any dating relationship, especially one leading to marriage. True and lasting love means developing a friendship, taking time to let the relationship develop, and building that relationship on a solid biblical foundation. There is a reason that Jesus taught that a wise man builds his house on the rock, while the foolish man builds his house on the sand (Luke 6:47–49). A relationship with Christ is the foundation on which all other marital factors should be built.

CHAPTER SEVEN

What's the Rush?

> But if we hope for what we do not
> yet have, we wait for it patiently.
>
> ROMANS 8:25

Why do so many people stampede into relationships? I have friends getting married left and right. Some have run to me with their ring fingers held high. Because I am not married, there are even those who've tried to make me feel like a piece of unclaimed luggage. After years of observing this stampede, I became curious. How did these people meet? How did their relationships develop so quickly? Far too many people are on a fast track to matrimony. If a relationship is within God's will, there is time to slow down and let that relationship develop. This is not just a good idea, it is critical.

Agape love, or unconditional love, is focused on another person without any thought of self. The Greek word *agape* describes the divine, selfless love that goes the extra mile to attain the well-being of the one loved. Knowing this, it is important that we take the time to understand the other person's heart. It is important to ask what is in his or her best interest, not for just today, but for the future. We must be willing to support that person, even if doing so conflicts with our own personal desires and goals.

It is difficult to really know a person's heart when you are lip-locked for hours and wrapped around each other like a pretzel. This is not love. It is *lust*! So what is the rush? From my observations, you should date someone at least one year before you consider marriage. Be patient and observe him or her in a wide range of activities, emotions, and situations. Remember, next to your determination to follow Jesus Christ, the choice of your spouse is the most important decision you will ever make.

Nobody enters into a marriage with the goal of getting divorced, and yet, many marriages fail. Why? Because too many people don't take the time to really get to know their intended well enough before they race down the aisle. This requires something that two people in love dread the most—*waiting*.

It is easy to live in a fairy tale world that blinds the two of you to the reality of the other person's character. You rarely get to know someone's true character in mere months because most of us put our best foot forward in the beginning. It is only once time marches on that all the dirt and grime become visible. I have a friend whose husband, during their dating years, always had the right thing to say to melt her heart. She used to joke that he must have a book that always gave him the right things to say. After they got married, however, those tender insights disappeared and her new joke became, "What happened to your book?"

Everyone is on their best behavior at first. They are charming, tender, compassionate, and self-sacrificing. During this period, it is easy to think, *This is the one!* But what about twelve months from now? Two years from now? Five? Every month you wait helps to reveal who this person really is.

Have you ever met someone and thought, *This person is really interesting and we seem to have so much in common. We click!?* So you spend time together. Over time, the red flags start to pop up. This person can't be open and honest with you. They lash out when things don't go their way. Instead of being a giver, your loved one turns out to be someone who takes and takes. Instead of feeling loved, you end up feeling used and abused. Given enough time, you may even find out you don't get along at all. Or maybe you'll discover that you have secret "triggers" that, despite your love for one another, drive you up the wall. That's why time is critical. Not only will it reveal a person's character, but it will reveal whether you have the skills needed to work through the inevitable relationship challenges in order to develop a healthy relationship.

In 1 Corinthians 13:4, Paul writes, "Love is patient." If you love this person, be patient. Think of a new relationship as being like a shiny, new car. When you first walk out of the showroom, you want to drive it everywhere and show it off. But slow down. Adhere to the speed limit. If you don't, your chances of getting into an accident are much greater. The same is true of dating. If you exceed the relationship speed limit, your chances of crashing are more probable. To put it humorously, the relationship starts out as ideal. Later on, it may become an ordeal. Before you know it, you are looking for a *new* deal!

All relationships take time to develop into what they will ultimately become—a disastrous wreck or something special. Give yourself the gift of time.

What Is Love…Really?

Giving yourself time is very difficult to do when you are in love. The tendency is to believe that "true love will conquer all." Theoretically, that's true. After all, Christ's love conquered all when He died on the cross. But as limited human beings, we have the tendency to overstate our emotions. We are quick to say that we "love," when what we really mean is that we are infatuated. Too often, we define love by the way we feel. "I can't imagine living without you." But this kind of "love" can fade with time or be shaken by circumstances.

True biblical love is defined as follows: "Love is patient, love is kind. It does not envy, it does not boast, it is not proud. It is not rude, it is not self-seeking, it is not easily angered, it keeps no record of wrongs. Love does not delight in evil but rejoices with the truth. It always protects, always trusts, always hopes, always perseveres. Love never fails" (1 Corinthians 13:4–8). This kind of love requires a conscious decision. It takes spiritual maturity. Can you imagine a love that is never rude, even when offended? A love that does not seek its own, even when treated unfairly? A love that keeps no record of wrongs, even over a period of years? This is truly a high standard, but it is the way that God intends us to love one another. If we let Him, He will help us do it. Keep this definition in mind the next time you are tempted to say you are "in love."

Now think about your intended spouse. Do you think that he or she can love *you* that same way? It is easy to say "yes" if you have only been together for a short time, but as time wears on, the real depth of this calling becomes clearer.

For these and many other reasons, giving your relationship time will give you either more confidence that this is the right person or more evidence that it is not now, nor ever will be, a healthy relationship. With time, you will see a person's true character. This will help you focus on becoming the person you need to be instead of focusing on what the other person should be for you.

Waiting Periods and Sex

One of the reasons that many Christians find it so difficult to wait for marriage is that they struggle with the Bible's command to abstain from premarital sex (1 Corinthians 6:18). Most Christians know this from the time they are young, and what do you think the typical response is? "I am so happy I have to wait until marriage for sexual intercourse!" Hardly! Most people are more likely to say, "God, why are You raining on my sexual parade? It is not fair!" This is because we fail to see the "why" behind God's prohibition, but believe it or not, it is for our own good.

Think about all the good things God does for us. We are made in His image. He has adopted us into His family and given us eternal life. He has given us the Holy Spirit. He has given us the Bible for guidance and direction. He has given us a body of believers for encouragement and support, and so much more. The prohibition on sex before marriage is part of His perfect wisdom and love. The marriage relationship is intended to reflect Christ's love for the Church, which is monogamous. Christ didn't have multiple partners before He chose us.

There is wisdom in the practical application, too. Ask married people who had premarital sex (whether with their spouse or someone else) whether, in hindsight, those sexual relationships were helpful to their marriage. If they are honest, most will tell you that they were not. Maybe a wife is jealous of a husband's past relationships and feels that she can't measure up. Maybe a husband becomes dissatisfied because he can't stop comparing his wife's bedroom style to someone else's. Whatever the baggage, it is always there. It will impact your marriage, whether you acknowledge it or not.

Abstaining from sex saves you from emotional pain as well. The heart is easily deceived. When you are in a sexual relationship, it becomes too easy to confuse the electricity of sex with true love. When sex sparks the relationship, many people think they are in love. After a few years of marriage, they may wake up and say, "Tell me again. Why did I marry you?" We date not to mate, but to find a lifetime companion. That requires a lot more than the emotions that swirl around sex.

This is why, when God wants us to wait until marriage for sex, He is helping us and not hindering us. I like what C.S. Lewis has to say about pleasure: It is God's invention, not the devil's. To this, many couples will respond, "But we are engaged. We know we're going to get married. What's the difference whether we have sex now or a few months from now?" Simple—obedience. That means no sex tonight. No sex on Valentine's night. No sex on engagement night or any other time until marriage.

We need to become lifemates before we are bedmates. Sexuality will flow from a lifelong commitment to marriage. Use this as a test of true love. Lust cannot wait. True love can. Make a promise to remain pure until you say "I do" before God.

CHAPTER EIGHT

Communication and Conflict

May the words of my mouth and the meditation of my heart
be pleasing in your sight, O Lord, my Rock and my Redeemer.

PSALM 19:14

G ood communication skills are one of the most important things
you can develop in order to maintain a successful relationship.
Without spoken words of love, care, and comfort, there is no relationship. Reuel Howe states, "Communication is to love what blood
is to the body. Take the blood out of the body and it dies."[3] Take
communication away from individuals and relationships die.

All relationships face the same basic issues, although at different levels, so what separates the great communicators from the
poor ones? The willingness to work at it daily. The willingness to
speak life into loved ones and tackle the task tenaciously. Those
who lack communication skills tend to just shrug their shoulders
and say, "Well, that's just the way it is." Sometimes, this is simply
because they fail to grasp its importance. Other times, it is due to
the frustration of not having the skills to improve it. The good
news is, anyone can learn to communicate. It is just a matter of
making it a priority.

Let's look at why good communication is such an important
skill to cultivate. Imagine that a woman has become frustrated by
her boyfriend's long hours at work. One day, she calls him to ask

---

[3] H. Norman Wright, *So You are Getting Married* (Ventura: Calif: Regal Books), 1985, p. 137.

if they are going to meet for dinner, but he tells her that he's going to work a little longer. She reacts angrily.

"*Again?*" she demands. "Don't you care about me at all?"

This is an example of poor communication. His working late might be a real issue in the relationship that needs to be addressed, but she is approaching it the wrong way. Because of the way she expressed her feelings, her boyfriend isn't going to hear a woman longing to be with the man she loves. Instead, he's going to hear the nagging and complaining of a woman who (he thinks) doesn't care about his job or the pressures of his life. In his mind, he is looking to create job security, build a nest egg, and solidify their future. And yet, all she can do is whine.

Instead of his heart being softened toward her, it hardens.

"All you do is complain," he shoots back. "You are never satisfied, and nothing is ever good enough for you."

Now she is *really* hurt. Although her words were taken as complaining and criticizing, what she really meant was, "Pay attention to me!" His response just made her feelings of being neglected that much worse.

Now imagine what might have happened if she had approached him differently. Instead of saying, "Don't you care about me at all?" what if she had said, "I know you work really hard and you have a lot of pressure on you. But I really miss you. If we can't have dinner together tonight, when can we?" Do you suppose his reaction might have been different?

Of course, even considering her complaints, his reaction wasn't any more sensitive (or godly). When she started criticizing, he could have said, "I know you are frustrated that I've been working a lot. I'm doing it because I love you and I'm trying to build a future for us. We'll get together this weekend and I'll make up for it. I promise."

Through good communication, either one of them could have averted the disaster this first interaction sparked.

Developing the Tools

To become a good communicator, you must first learn to listen. This means more than just hearing words. Truly *listening* demands that you lend the person your heart. It means that you absorb and really understand what is being said. That includes what's *not* being said. Sometimes you have to read between the lines.

So what stops you from really understanding what your loved one is trying to say? What draws your attention away when he or she is talking? Do you glance around to see who walked in? Are you absorbed in your own problems? Maybe you are in a defensive mode, only listening long enough to formulate what you are going to shoot back in response. Or maybe you are in the habit of continually turning the conversation back to yourself.

That is not listening. It's hearing. Listening means hearing what others are saying and taking a genuine interest in it. If you monopolize the conversation or focus only on your own agenda, you learn nothing. It was once said that there is a reason we have two ears and one mouth. We should do twice as much listening as we do talking!

Listening also requires feeling empathy toward the one who is speaking. It means you are trying to understand the true feelings being communicated. Listening is close to the heart of God. When you listen, you love. James 1:19 says, "My dear brothers, take note of this: Everyone should be quick to listen, slow to speak and slow to become angry." When you do this, you reveal how much you care about the other person.

Next time your loved one wants to talk, remember that listening and hearing are two different things. *Hearing* helps you gain content or information. In the context of a relationship, when you are only hearing, you are more concerned about what *you* think and *you* feel. When you truly *listen*, you develop a heartfelt understanding of what the other person is trying to say. When you don't incorporate listening and hearing together, your relationship will suffer.

Now for the Rest of the Story...

Of course, listening is only half of good communication. This is because it is not just what comes in that matters (listening), but what goes out. In other words, you must also respond well. Why? Just look at the example above. Words are like high-powered octane. They have the power to energize a relationship or the power to kill it. Using the right words in the right way will grow a relationship. Using the wrong words in the wrong way can kill it. Your timing, context, and tone are rarely, if ever, neutral. They will either build or destroy.

A husband asks his wife, "Did you remember to get coffee at the store?"

"No," she says. "I'm sorry. I forgot."

"Of *course* you did," he says, his words dripping like acid. "You always do."

Inside, a little bit of his wife just died.

Good communication goes beyond words, as well. What is your body language saying? When someone else is speaking, are you looking them in the eyes, showing respect and concern? Are you nodding, letting her know that you are listening? Are you asking appropriate questions, indicating that you are trying to understand? Or are you paying more attention to the text messages on your cell phone?

Women, there is a cautionary tale here. Just because you are a woman doesn't mean that you automatically communicate well. Culturally, we tend to think of women as the better communicators. We think of them as listening, hearing, and responding to their partners, while men are clueless and insensitive rubes. However, when I queried a number of singles and married couples, both men and women complained that their loved ones have issues with communication.

What's the problem? Men tend to allow their pride or egos to stand in the way of expressing their true feelings. Many would rather be flattened by a tractor-trailer than have a serious heart-to-heart talk. Women, on the other hand, often take forever to get to the point. We beat around the bush, repeat ourselves, and recite what seem to men to be endless stories before we get down to business. Sometimes, we do not reveal our honest feelings because we want to avoid any possibility of conflict or rejection. Other times, we tend to criticize and complain more than we realize.

Such poor communication skills result in serious conflict, especially over time. So how do *you* handle such quarrels? Do you talk about them? Do you listen carefully and consider the other person's point of view? Do you apologize quickly when you are wrong? (You are wrong sometimes, aren't you?) Do you lash out in anger or do you keep it inside like a smoldering fire, letting the flames of bitterness and hurt consume you?

Years ago, I dated a man with whom I would start fights on a regular basis. I broke up with him over and over. Every time, we patched our differences and ended up back together. Every time, I started another argument. One day, he looked at me and said, "I'm not playing this game anymore." He meant it—we didn't get back together again. I was devastated. While alone in my apartment, I had plenty of time to think. God uses experiences like this to drive us to our knees in prayer, and that's exactly what happened to me. With a profound desire to change, I turned to the Lord and asked, "Why am I so ugly in my attitude and actions toward others?" God revealed how much bitterness and unforgiveness I had living in my heart. When I began to work through all of it, I realized that I had been a slave to sin, but through Christ, I had become free. "So if the Son sets you free, you will be free indeed" (John 8:36). The battle I'd been fighting was won through Christ.

James 4:1–3 addresses these battles. "What causes fights and quarrels among you? Don't they come from your desires that battle within you? You want something but don't get it. You kill and covet, but you cannot have what you want. You quarrel and fight. You do not have, because you do not ask God. When you ask, you do not receive, because you ask with wrong motives, that you may spend what you get on your pleasures."

This describes the root cause of destructive conflict. Conflicts arise from unforgiveness, disappointment, and unmet desire. Good communication has the opposite effect. It bonds two people and deepens intimacy.

Preparing for the Inevitable

In relationships, strife is inevitable. We are all human beings, fallen and sinful, and in any relationship, there will be times when a line is drawn and sides are taken. In different areas, all of us have clashing viewpoints. It is important that we don't hold a grudge, keep a record of wrongs, or hold onto unforgiveness. These things are sin, and Christ died to set us free from sin.

There will also be times of misunderstanding, and you must commit to working through them. Conflicts should never be buried. That just allows them to build, either to explode later or manifest themselves in a different way. Instead, be committed to resolving those conflicts, even if it is agreeing to disagree once mutual understanding is reached. You can do that by using the right words, in the right way, and with the right actions. The goal is to move to shared understanding.

Each of us communicates differently, responds to problems differently, and even apologizes differently. Even so, this is not an excuse for poor behavior. Every relationship will have arguments, but arguments can be either cruel and crushing or they can be creative and constructive. Cruel conflict is mounted like a war to inflict pain and suffering. It twists resolvable disputes into damaging battles, breaking down relationships. Creative conflict translates struggles into deepened commitment. It seeks to understand where the other person is coming from and, in the end, works to build one another up.

10

Of course, in our selfishness, we don't always want creative, constructive conflict. Sometimes, we just want to lash out. We don't care how the other person feels about it. We don't want to phrase it correctly. Our emotions are raw and we just want to be heard. In the short term, this makes us feel better, but it does not solve anything. In fact, it makes the situation worse. A verbal wound is as bad as a physical one. Both can occur in a matter of seconds and take a long time to heal, if they heal at all. More often, one verbal wound is inflicted upon another so that, over time, you are driven even further apart.

If you truly want to grow the relationship, never attack the other person. Speak the truth in love instead of raising your voice, criticizing, or putting the other person down. A wise man once said, "How does destroying your neighbor's house make your house any better?" In relationships, how does negative talk make anyone's life any better—yours or theirs? In Ephesians 4:29, Paul exhorts us, "Do not let any unwholesome talk come out of your mouths, but only what is helpful for building others up according to their needs, that it may benefit those who listen." In verse 31, it goes on to say, "Get rid of all bitterness, rage and anger, brawling and slander, along with every form of malice."

If you concentrate solely on negative issues, you may win the battle, but you could lose the relationship. If you keep your focus on God, it will be reflected in your actions, words, and deeds, and the battle will be won.

Get Over Your PMS

If I had to sum up why there is so much tension in today's marriages, it would be three things: PMS. No, not *that* PMS! **P**oor communication, **M**oney, and **S**ex. But even money and sex can be dealt with if you have good communication. So let's look at some basic principles for resolving conflict and communicating effectively.

1. Stick to the point.

When you are hurt and angry, it is too easy to start drifting. You bring up this issue and that issue, and past arguments. All this does is blow the problem out of proportion. You might get into name-calling, threats, and irrelevant issues that undermine the relationship instead of deepen it.

I know a couple in which the husband's dislike for his wife's parents is a major source of conflict. In nearly every fight, he brings up a litany of complaints about them, and when she tries to address each specific accusation, the discussion gets derailed. The original issue never gets addressed, let alone resolved. Gradually, she began to resist the temptation to defend every attack. Now, she says things like, "I understand how you feel about my parents, but this issue concerns *us* and how *we* are going to handle [whatever it might be]…" Soon, she began to find that the conflicts were getting shorter and they reached resolutions on the narrower, more specific issues.

2. Don't bring up the past.

Unless it is immediately relevant to the discussion, don't bring up the past (Isaiah 43:18). This doesn't mean that you never mention things that have happened. It means that once you have talked about something or the other person has apologized for it, it is done. We are to forgive others as God forgives us. How does God forgive? He puts our sins as far from us as the east is from the west and remembers them no more (Psalm 103:12; Isaiah 43:25). If you need to bring up past actions in order to make a point or establish a pattern, that's okay. But if you find yourself harboring bitterness over an infraction and bringing it up over and over, it becomes your problem, not the other person's.

3. Don't talk negatively or criticize.

When you have a conflict, talk about solving the problem and stick to the point. For example, if your loved one always walks into your home with muddy boots, don't say, "You are such a slob! Why can't you remember to take your shoes off?" That is a criticism and attack. Instead, try something like, "Even though I've asked repeatedly, you keep tracking mud on the floor. What can we do so that you remember to take your shoes off when you come in?" This focuses on the problem, not the person. Not only is this approach more glorifying to God, but your loved one is less likely to be defensive and therefore more likely to be open to coming up with solutions. Sure, it takes effort to change the way you talk, but it is worth it!

4. Go to God for the answers.

It would be great if every problem had a nice, neat solution, but that's not the way it works. Sometimes, resolution takes time. Fortunately, even when you don't have the answers, God does. So in the middle of a conflict, instead of relying on your own wisdom, immediately turn to God. James 1:5 says, "If any of you lacks wisdom, he should ask God, who gives generously to all without finding fault, and it will be given to him." Sometimes, God's answers aren't the easiest or don't feel the best to implement, but they are always the right ones.

5. Let God do the changing.

It is never your job to try to change someone else. Nor is it your job to teach your loved ones the right way to do things or to punish them when they do wrong ("I'm not going to call her for a week!" Or, "I can't believe he said that. Now I'm not going to go to that barbeque with him!"). When you do this, you try to take the place of God Himself. The result is only more conflict and unrest.

It is God's job to fix that person, not yours. Change will happen only once that person *desires* to change and allows God to do the work in his or her heart. In the meantime, your job is to extend forgiveness, release him or her to God, and allow God to do the work.

By releasing the responsibility to God (where it belongs anyway), you will experience freedom, peace, and a more intimate relationship with God and others.

6. Focus on others, not yourself.

Selfishness is an unwholesome characteristic that can—and will—destroy relationships. The only way we can combat selfishness is by choosing every day to serve someone other than ourselves. Once again, this means giving up our rights and yielding them to God. For example, how are you doing in the area of self-sacrifice? Would you be willing to give up what you want to help a person in need? Or are you so wrapped up in your own problems that you can't see the needs of others? If we are to fight against the destructive force of selfishness, we must be willing to prepare now by choosing to serve those around us so that God can begin to reshape our character. Philippians 2:3-4 says, "Do nothing out of selfish ambition or vain conceit, but in humility consider others better than yourselves. Each of you should look not only to your own interests, but also to the interests of others."

Sometimes this selfishness is difficult to see. We may think we spend our lives helping others, but we fail to realize that we are helping *who* we want, *when* we want, and *how* we want. True selflessness involves sacrifices we don't want to make. For example, it might be easy to give up a golf game to win the affection of your new girlfriend by changing the oil in her car. But when she asks you to drive her brother (whom you can't stand) back to college three hours away, you'd rather be dead than spend that much time with him. But that's the true test of sacrifice—when it hurts.

Another place it is difficult to see selfishness is during conflict. Often, we are more interested in looking for someone else's flaws than our own. The following is an example of a conflict that has probably occurred in every household, at some time, in some form or another:

A man comes home from work. His wife chose to stay home with the children, but she also continues to telecommute to her old job part-time. She is home all day, caring for the children, taking care of the house, and planning the meals, while also working 15–20 hours per week. She has had a frustrating day. The children are fussy and sick. The dog vomited on the carpet. The baby is screaming. The toddler is about to toss an iPod down the stairs. She hasn't gotten a lick of work done and she has a deadline in the morning.

Her husband walks in, goes to get a drink from the refrigerator, and notices that the barbeque sauce from leftovers that spilled on the shelf two nights ago still hasn't been cleaned up. He, too, has had a frustrating day. The boss didn't like his presentation. His co-worker is on her honeymoon, so he is doing both his work and hers. The air conditioning isn't working in the car—again—and it is 90 degrees outside. Now the car is making that knocking sound again. All he wants is a cold drink, but the sight of that two-day-old spill churns his stomach.

"Why is this still in here?" he snaps. "I thought you were going to clean it up."

She responds with sarcasm. "In case you hadn't noticed, I haven't exactly had time."

"Why not?" he says. "You're home all day. It would only take five minutes."

"Fine," she snaps back. "If it would only take five minutes, then *you* do it!"

He slams the refrigerator door. "Boy, that was rude. You need to watch your mouth."

Needless to say, this erupts into a full-blown fight, with each person focusing on the failings of the other person. He complains that she spends more time working than the 15 hours per week she promised, and now the household responsibilities are suffering. She rants about his lack of understanding about the other responsibilities on her shoulders, too, and the pressures she faces every day. Neither is aware of the real problem at hand, which is the fact that both people are focusing entirely on their own problems and their own agendas.

Although we don't often think of it this way, this is selfishness in its most deceptive form. After all, what did Jesus say about our tendency to focus on someone else's failings rather than our own? "Why do you look at the speck of sawdust in your brother's eye and pay no attention to the plank in your own eye? How can you say to your brother, 'Let me take the speck out of your eye,' when all the time there is a plank in your own eye?" (Matthew 7:3–4). Pulling out our own planks is very difficult to do, especially when we feel that we have been offended. But Jesus is very clear. We are to focus on our own sins, not the sins of others.

Points to Recall

In closing, let's look at some final scriptural principles that will help us become better communicators.

1. Think before you speak (Proverbs 15:23).
2. Choose your words carefully (Proverbs 16:24).
3. Connect instead of correct (Philippians 2:1–5).
4. Remember that how you speak is as important as what you say (Proverbs 18:21).
5. Use words to build up instead of destroy (Ephesians 4:29).
6. Check your motives by talking to the Lord first (Proverbs 16:2).

If you were to employ all of these principles each time conflict arises, how do you think it might affect your relationships with those close to you? It might seem like a lot to remember at first, but over time, it becomes second nature. So does the closeness and intimacy that this kind of communication creates.

CHAPTER NINE

Learning to Forgive

Then Peter came and said to Him, "Lord, how often shall my brother
sin against me and I forgive him? Up to seven times?" Jesus said to him,
"I do not say to you, up to seven times, but up to seventy times seven."

MATTHEW 18:21–22 NASB

I f you wrote a list of people who have hurt you and then a list
of people whom you have hurt, which list do you think would
be longer? In my counseling sessions, I am amazed at how many
people say, "It is the people I have hurt." If this is your answer,
let me ask you a question. Which list do you dwell on the most?
Those whom you have hurt? Or those who have hurt you? More
than likely, it is the latter. We can easily recall how others have
mistreated us, but we quickly forget (or don't even realize) how
we have offended others. In fact, we can say we forgive even as
we continue to hang onto bitterness, anger, and pain.

Steps Toward Forgiveness

In this chapter, we will look at a series of steps you can take to
help you through the forgiveness process. First, however, I want
to stress that true reconciliation does not start with human effort,
not even from those who hurt you.

Forgiveness is not something we can achieve on our own. How
many times have you desired an apology, but the person wasn't
willing to give it? How often has someone asked you for forgiveness, but you weren't willing to offer it? How many times has
someone offered an apology, but you weren't ready to accept it?

That's why, before looking at the steps toward forgiveness, it is important to recognize that all forgiveness comes through Christ. That means it *starts* with Christ.

Often, we lash out in anger because we are looking for the other person to heal the wounds they inflicted, but they can't. Healing our hearts is a job that only God can do. That's why, when you have been injured, you need to go to Christ first. Bring *Him* your hurt and pain. Allow *Him* to heal you. Only once your heart has been healed can you truly reconcile with your loved one. Because Jesus granted you forgiveness and healing, you can now freely grant it to others. Ephesians 4:32 says, "Be kind and compassionate to one another, forgiving each other, just as in Christ God forgave you."

But going to God for healing is often the last thing on our minds. This is why, when many people experience the end of a relationship, they are tempted to jump right into another one. We are looking for someone else to heal the hurts from the past. If only we can find someone new to love, we think that hurt and emptiness will go away. This is only a temporary and superficial solution. The reality is, all of us need to give God time to heal our hearts—truly heal them—before we move into a new relationship. Otherwise, we'll end up bringing that hurt into another relationship, often in destructive ways.

Learning Forgiveness

Okay, forgiveness sounds good. But it is not easy to do. Although many people readily admit they need to forgive, they also admit they aren't very good at forgiving. Part of the reason is they don't know how. Merely thinking about forgiveness doesn't cause it to happen. Hurts can be very deep and the pain overwhelming. Forgiveness has to be a willful, conscious act. So how do you learn to forgive?

Let's look at some practical steps you can take.

1. Identify and isolate the problem.

Before you can forgive anything, you need to be able to identify exactly what it is that you are forgiving. Think back to the chapter on communication and conflict. Remember the woman who complains that her boyfriend doesn't care about her at all? This kind of hurt and feeling of rejection is so generalized that it is difficult to forgive. Narrow it down. What is the *specific* offense? Her boyfriend frequently works late and doesn't take her feelings into account. This is far different and more manageable than, "He doesn't care about me." Isolating the offense allows you to focus on a specific issue, not the person, and effectively deal with what's going on.

2. Turn to God—not the offender—for healing.

Too often, we expect the person who committed the offense to be the one to take away the pain. While this sounds reasonable, no human being can do that. Even if they could, what if they weren't willing to do so? Or what if the person's best effort doesn't meet your expectations? No human being can be responsible for the pain we are carrying. Even if the offender does acknowledge wrongdoing, God must still be the first and foremost source of our healing.

3. Admit that it hurts.

Be able to identify with the emotions going on inside of you. Tell Jesus that it hurts. It sounds simple, but we often try to bury our pain. We think it is easier to push those feelings down or ignore them. By doing so, we hope they will go away. We are fooling ourselves. There is an old saying, "Time heals all wounds," but this isn't always true. Time heals all wounds *only if it is accompanied by forgiveness*. Without forgiveness, that pain only takes root. Sometimes, it results in hardness of heart. Other times, it just festers. So the next step in forgiveness is admitting that you are hurting.

4. Take responsibility, where appropriate.

Next, we must accept our part in the wrongdoing. Occasionally, an offense is one way, but it is rare. More often, we played a part in it somehow. Maybe she said something to set him off. Maybe he said something insensitive, but she magnified it and started a big fight. Whatever our role, we must take responsibility.

Confess to God your own imperfection. Repent for any sinful reactions on your end. Be aware, however, that God may lead you to ask for forgiveness, too. In Matthew 5:23–24, Jesus says, "Therefore, if you are offering your gift at the altar and there remember that your brother has something against you, leave your gift there in front of the altar. First go and be reconciled to your brother; then come and offer your gift." Asking for forgiveness when you feel that *you* have been offended is very difficult, but it is part of God's plan for reconciliation and growth.

5. Release the debt.

Once you have done all that God has asked of you—isolating the offense, taking responsibility for the role you played in the incident, and asking for forgiveness, if necessary, then let go and leave the offender in God's hands. Tell God that you choose to no longer hold onto the hurt and allow Him to work in the situation in His way. Remember, once Jesus forgives us, He no longer holds us guilty before Him (Romans 8:1). Our sins are wiped clean and He remembers them no more (Isaiah 43:25; Hebrews 10:17). If God can do that for us, we are to extend the same to others. We are to forgive as the Lord forgave us. We release the right to hold onto bitterness and anger or punish the offender somehow. Their debt to us has been fulfilled through Christ.

6. Trust God with the outcome.

This is perhaps the hardest part of forgiveness. If we really think about it, one of the reasons we don't forgive is that we don't trust God. We don't trust that He knows what He is doing. We don't trust Him to use these situations for our good and His glory (Romans 8:28). We don't trust Him to bring justice. We don't trust that He is loving by allowing us to go through such pain. Therefore, holding onto resentment is our way of rebelling. Instead of yielding and humbling ourselves to His sovereign will, we lash out, manipulate, and try to exert control. In some ways, unforgiveness is a form of self-pity. Trusting God is a critical component in the ability to forgive.

Making the Choice

We all have the capacity to forgive, but forgiveness is a choice. It is a courageous one. In fact, it is the most courageous act in which you can participate. You can make a choice to separate the offender from his or her deed and purposefully decide to forgive and release the negative feelings you harbor. It is not a position of weakness, but a position of strength.

"But Emily," you might say, "you don't know how badly I have been hurt." Oh, but I do. I've had my share of anguish, and I know all too well the devastation that comes from unforgiveness. I used to enter into a relationship, and after a few months, we would split up and go our separate ways. I felt wounded and refused to forgive. Instead, I stuffed my wounded feelings and emotions. Then I would jump into another relationship, trying to forget the previous one. In time, however, the raw pain would be exposed and reveal itself in my attitudes and behaviors. I became controlling. Maybe a boyfriend promised to do something, but he didn't follow through. Later, that unforgiveness came out in my attempts to control the next person to make him do what I wanted him to do. I had to keep an eye on him because the last one let me down.

Destructive cycles like these do not stop until you determine to forgive. When I finally made the choice, I experienced true freedom. I became free from past hurts. I no longer held my former boyfriends guilty before me. They were still responsible before God for their choices (just as I was responsible for mine), but I released all right to hold onto that hurt or to require payment for it.

If you are in a relationship—any relationship—you will experience pain. Even the most well-intentioned people will fail you sometimes. You will fail others, too. If the two of you don't learn how to handle those failures in a healthy way, you can end up in destructive cycles that spiral out of control. The emotional devastation does not go away on its own. It only grows over time and becomes a major reason for divorce. It is one of the reasons it is so important to forgive, whether you feel like it or not.

Let's review those six steps toward forgiveness again:

1. Identify and isolate the problem.
2. Turn to God—not the offender—for healing.
3. Admit that it hurts.
4. Take responsibility where appropriate.
5. Release the debt.
6. Trust God with the outcome.

Try practicing them next time you are hurt or offended. You might be surprised how well they work.

Have You *Really* Forgiven?

You may think you have forgiven those around you, but have you really? A lot of us think we have forgiven when, in fact, we have only covered over our resentment. There were times I thought I had forgiven until the Lord revealed to me that I was continuing to play the blame game for some real or imagined wrong. In my effort to get a person or a problem off my mind, I was actually clinging *tighter* to bitterness and hurt. Instead of focusing on God's truth—that forgiveness is a choice—I was allowing the situation and circumstances to control me.

My years as a Christian counselor have been a real eye-opener because I've had a chance to see the long-term consequences of unforgiveness many times over. The more I began to see its devastating effects, the more I saw the need to forgive in my own life. It motivated me to release my pent-up emotions and concentrate entirely on God and His Word. I no longer sought my completeness in someone else. Instead, I discovered that God is truly sufficient for all of my needs. He is my Friend, my Healer, my Lover, and my Companion. He is all I need. Once I truly understood this, forgiveness came more easily because I was no longer asking the person who hurt me to be responsible for my healing. Only then was I able to experience the fruit of the Spirit: love, joy, peace, patience, kindness, goodness, faithfulness, gentleness, and self-control (Galatians 5:22–23).

So have you truly forgiven someone? Test yourself and see:

1. Have you released your right to hold onto anger, bitterness, and hurt?
2. Are you sincerely thanking God for the lessons learned during the pain (Romans 8:28–29)?
3. Can you talk about your hurt without getting angry, without feeling resentful, without the slightest thought of revenge (Ephesians 4:31)?
4. Do you have a willingness to accept your part of the blame for what happened?
5. Can you revisit the scene or the person(s) involved in your hurt without experiencing a negative reaction?
6. Are you rewarding with good those who have hurt you (Romans 12:20–21)? [4]

---

[4] *Life Ministry Manual*, Victorious Christian Living International, Inc., 1999, Diagram 200-G.

If you can honestly answer "yes" to all of these questions, then true forgiveness has taken place. If you have answered "no" to any of them, I strongly encourage you to go to the Lord and resolve the issue in your heart. Turn your "no" into "yes."

Consequences of Unforgiveness

What happens when you don't forgive? There are three primary consequences I want to discuss.

First, unforgiveness is like a piece of fruit rotting in the refrigerator. The longer it stays there, the more rotten it gets. It may look good on the outside, but on the inside, it is molding and fermenting. If we don't forgive, we will be like that piece of fruit. Bitterness will continue to poison us.

Second, unforgiveness can cause problems, not only with those with whom we have relationships, but also with those whom we haven't even met. I recall times when I met someone who was eerily similar to someone with whom I was upset. The person either had the same job title, the same name, the same personality, or even looked like that person. Inadvertently, I found myself harboring negative thoughts and emotions, even though this person had caused me no harm. As a result, I missed out on some wonderful relationships.

Third, unforgiveness always harms us more than the other person. In fact, someone once said that bitterness is like drinking poison and waiting for the other person to die. Not only does our unforgiveness destroy our current relationships, but it is not pleasing to God. As followers of Christ, we are commanded to forgive. Colossians 3:13 says, "Bear with each other and forgive whatever grievances you may have against one another. Forgive as the Lord forgave you." When the Lord forgave us, He forgave a big debt. Not just one offense, or even a dozen, but *all* of our offenses, both seen and unseen, committed every day of our lives. He made that sacrifice before even one of those sins occurred (Romans

5:8). Can you imagine sacrificing everything you have, everything you desire, even your very life, for someone who doesn't even realize or appreciate it? This is what Christ did for us.

Our willingness to forgive others is a small sacrifice in light of what Jesus has done for us. When I choose to forgive, I release the power of God in my life. I experience true joy and happiness in Christ and in all my earthly relationships. When I keep focused on Him, I can face the truth about my emotions and be at peace because Jesus can help me overcome anything, if only I allow Him.

In this, we might consider the frustrations in our relationships as a wonderful gift from God. Yes, a gift! He gave us a free will and allows us to make mistakes if we so choose. When we allow Him to do surgery on our hearts, we become dissatisfied with worldly pleasures and pursue Him. This is where true joy and lasting happiness lie. Yes, true joy is not found in dating relationships, marriage, or anything else. Permanent, everlasting, and fulfilling joy is only found in an authentic relationship with Jesus Christ. Sometimes, we only learn this when other relationships fail us, but it's a lesson worth learning.

Conclusion

The reason I became a counselor was to help people. One of the areas where people need the most help is in relationships, especially relationships leading to marriage. The reason I wrote this book was to take the lessons learned from those years of counseling and multiply them to help even more people avoid the most common relationship mistakes.

In these pages, I have discussed the issues that I have seen come up over and over again. If you ask me to sum up the most *important* mistake, however, it is that people think that marriage will fill a void in their lives. If only they find "the one," they think the emptiness will go away. This fundamental misunderstanding propels them into a rushed decision rather than allowing the relationship to develop and dealing with any unresolved issues before committing to a lifetime.

To all of the singles reading this book, I want to emphasize that nobody—*nobody*—can fill the God-shaped void in your heart. If you are considering marriage, make sure that neither of you is depending on the other person for fulfillment. That fulfillment must come from God, and only from God, or you will end up misplacing your needs onto someone who cannot fulfill them. No matter how wonderful your significant other may be, he or she is still human and will fail you eventually. Probably more than once. That's why your most passionate relationship must be with your Heavenly Father. The more you fall in love with Christ, the fewer demands you will place on your future spouse and the freer you will be to love him or her with true agape love.

If you are already in a relationship with one whom you believe is the right person, begin to critically evaluate the relationship in ways you may never have done. It is my hope that the principles put forth in this book will help you. Even though this is not an exhaustive look at all of the problems a couple may face, I hope that you will learn from them so that you *don't* end up in my counseling office—or anyone else's for that matter.

We have discussed a lot of principles throughout this book. To help pull them together, here are some questions to consider about yourself and your potential spouse that will help you prepare for that big day.

1. What is my real motive behind dating this person? Am I dating to fill a void in my life that only God can fill?
2. Is our relationship centered on Christ? Or one another?
3. Am I setting a spiritual example in this relationship?
4. Am I in the relationship for what I can get? Or what I can give?
5. Is this relationship drawing me closer to God or further away from Him?
6. What kind of baggage am I carrying into the relationship? Or has my baggage been checked at the foot of the cross?
7. Have I developed healthy ways to deal with the hurts and conflicts that will inevitably arise when sharing a life with someone else?

If any of these issues prove to be real challenges for you, I encourage you to commit to high-quality Christian counseling before setting a wedding date. Whether it is a pastor or a trained Christian counselor, get help. Yes, these issues are that important.

Conclusion

Celebrate Singleness

As you continue on your journey, you may realize that finding your intended mate is more difficult than you'd thought. Maybe it will take much longer than you expected. That's okay. *The right person is worth waiting for.* In the meantime, it is all right to be single. Celebrate it! You have more freedom, more time, and more opportunities than someone who is married. Remember Paul's admonition about marriage: "But those who marry will face many troubles in this life, and I want to spare you this" (1 Corinthians 7:28). There is a reason he said this.

Marriage carries burdens and responsibilities—as well as infinite joys—all its own. Marriage was designed by God to be a joyful experience, but He did not design it to be like a fairy tale in which two people see one another from across a crowded room, meet, and ride off into the sunset to live happily ever after. God designed marriage as a tool to bless us, but also to refine us, grow us, and conform us to the image of His Son. This is a fulfilling process, but it is not an easy one.

I hear some people say: "But I *need* to get married." "I *need* someone to spend time with." "I won't feel complete without children." This is the wrong attitude. Too many singles are focused on what they don't have instead of what they *do* have. Your single years are precious. They are your opportunity to serve God, both in your singleness and in your preparation to be a better wife or husband. It is precious time that you will never get back. Enjoy it.

As you continue your search for your perfect mate, keep in mind God's ideal marriage relationship, outlined in Ephesians 5:22–28: "Wives, submit to your husbands as to the Lord. For the husband is the head of the wife as Christ is the head of the church, his body, of which he is the Savior. Now as the church submits to Christ, so also wives should submit to their husbands in everything. Husbands, love your wives, just as Christ loved the church and gave himself up for her to make her holy, cleansing

85

her by the washing with water through the word, and to present her to himself as a radiant church, without stain or wrinkle or any other blemish, but holy and blameless. In this same way, husbands ought to love their wives as their own bodies. He who loves his wife loves himself."

These are difficult commands, and when you consider that this is the model God set forth, it will separate out the casual relationships from the godly ones. Do you trust this person enough to submit to him as unto the Lord? Even when he refuses to see your point of view? Do you trust her enough to lay your life down for her in everything? To put her first, even if you don't get what you feel you deserve in return?

When you are ready to love someone this way, then you are ready to consider marriage. When you find the person to whom you can entrust your life under these conditions, rejoice! You will be entering an exciting and immensely fulfilling season of your life. If not, rejoice anyway! God intends marriage to be blissful, but if you get married before you are ready, it will be a rocky road. Unlike other bad decisions, you can't just walk away from this one. So rejoice that God has given us a clear picture of His plan so we can make smart choices before we make that leap.

In all things, rejoice. If you are waiting for marriage, rejoice that He will give us everything we need to find the perfect mate to accomplish His will for our lives. As you are waiting, rejoice He has also given us everything we need for a joyful, fulfilling life, even as a single person. "'For I know the plans I have for you,' declares the Lord, 'plans to prosper you and not to harm you, plans to give you hope and a future'" (Jeremiah 29:11).

Waiting for "the right one" can be hard, but there is no better promise to hold onto while you are waiting.

The Free Gift

If someone hands you a gift, what are you most likely to say? "No, thank you. I couldn't!" Hardly! You are much more likely to say, "Great! Thanks!"

Did you know that someone has already given you a gift? Not just any gift, but the greatest gift you could ever receive? It is the gift of eternal life. You didn't earn it. You didn't deserve it. Like a newborn baby who can't earn the love she is given and yet is showered with adoration, God gave us this gift for no reason other than because He loves us.

But like any gift, God's greatest gift is useless unless we unwrap it. God granted this gift to the entire world, but only those who open the gift will receive the blessings it contains. Have you unwrapped this free gift? If not, would you like to do so? If your answer is yes, then read on!

Have You Offended God?

The Bible says that when we sin (and we all do), we offend God. "For all have sinned and fall short of the glory of God" (Romans 3:23) and "the wages of sin is death" (Romans 6:23), or eternal separation from God. As difficult as this is to think about, it means that we all deserve to spend an eternity in hell separated from God.

Some may protest, saying, "I'm not worried. I'm not as bad as all that. There are lots of people who are worse than me." That may be true, but God doesn't grade on a curve. The Bible says that all of us have failed God, and for this reason, none of us is immune from the curse of sin and death.

You see, once we sin, we can't take that sin back. Just like when one partner is unfaithful to another, there is nothing we can *do* to erase it from our past. You may think, "But I'm a good person. God wouldn't send me to hell." It doesn't matter how good we are. God's standard is perfection. Are you perfect? I know I'm not. For this reason, the Bible says that nothing is "good enough" to earn us eternal life.

So how do we get into heaven? We must receive God's forgiveness. For this to happen, we need a Savior—Jesus. To receive His salvation, you must recognize that you are a sinner and can do nothing to save yourself. Isaiah 53:6 says, "We all, like sheep, have gone astray, each of us has turned to his own way; and the Lord has laid on him the iniquity of us all." Just as a drowning man cannot save himself but needs someone to pull him out, we need Jesus to pull us out of the hopeless situation we are in.

Accepting the Gift

How do we receive this free gift? *Simply by trusting in Jesus.* When we trust Jesus as our Savior, our sins are forgiven. Not just one sin or most of our sins, but all of them. Once our sins are forgiven, we are given the gift of eternal life. This is God's gift to us, not because of anything we have done, but because of what Jesus has done. Salvation is a gift that can only be received, never earned. If you had to earn it, it wouldn't be a gift. Ephesians 2:8-9 says, "For it is by grace you have been saved, through faith—and this not from yourselves, it is the gift of God—not by works, so that no one can boast."

This gift is available to us any time we ask. We must simply recognize our helplessness before God, confess that we have sinned and fallen short of His perfection, and repent of our sins. We must admit that we need His help to live a life that is pleasing to Him. This help comes in the form of Jesus, who died on the cross for our sins. We must believe that He is Lord of the universe and of our lives, and that God raised Him from the dead (Romans 10:9). Once we pray this, we trust that Jesus will forgive us and take us to heaven.

Some people will say, "This is too confusing. I just don't know what to pray." It doesn't really matter what words you use. It is not the prayer itself that saves you. It is faith that Jesus will forgive your sins and take you to heaven. But if you are searching for words, let me suggest the following prayer. You can change it around if you want, or you can pray it as it is written and let it be a simple expression of the faith that is in your heart:

> *Dear Jesus, I believe in You. I believe that You are the Son of God and You died for my sins. I believe God has raised You from the dead and that You are Lord of all creation. Please forgive me for all my sins. Cleanse my heart with Your precious blood. I trust You now as my Lord and Savior. Thank You, Lord! In Your name I pray. Amen!*

If you just sincerely prayed this prayer, *congratulations!* You are now a child of God, a new creature in Christ (2 Corinthians 5:17). You have just unwrapped and taken hold of the most important gift you could ever receive.

Using the Gift

Some people think that once they accept God's gift of salvation, that's it. They don't have to do anything else. While it is true that God's gift of eternal life is free, there is a lot more to His gift than we realize.

After all, once you receive a gift, do you just stare at the box and admire the wrapping paper? Of course not. You open the gift and enjoy it. If it's a piece of jewelry, you wear it. If it's an electronic gadget, you see what it can do. God's gift of salvation is even better. Once we accept this gift, God does a supernatural work in our hearts. He changes our nature into one that desires to serve and please Him. He gives us His Holy Spirit, who teaches us and empowers us to do things we couldn't do before. If we ask, He freely offers us His wisdom to guide and direct our lives.

In other words, *if we use the gift*, we release God's supernatural power. Are you frustrated by how to resolve a conflict with your loved one? You could do what you *think* is the right thing and you might even get the result you are looking for, but you might make a mess of things too. Or you might think you got it right, only to find out later that it had long-term consequences you didn't anticipate. In reality, the "right" thing often depends on things we don't know anything about, such as what someone else is thinking or feeling, events that are going on behind the scenes, or how decisions will impact the course of future events. As human beings, we see only part of the picture. This is why our decisions can so easily be wrong.

Who has the whole picture? Who sees the end from the beginning? God. That's why He has the ability to offer perfect wisdom and the right solution each time. Whose wisdom would you rather trust? Yours or His?

Accessing God's Wisdom

But that wisdom doesn't just drop out of the box. It is something that is cultivated from a relationship with God. It's like, when you first meet someone, you think you know them. But the only way to truly know someone is to spend time with them. It's the same with God. The more time we spend with Him, the more easily we can discern His will for our lives. That's why, once we open the gift, God's desire is not that we set it on a shelf, but that we open it and use it. This requires growing in our Christian faith and making a daily decision to follow Jesus.

In Luke 9:23, Jesus says, "If anyone would come after me, he must deny himself and take up his cross daily and follow me." As a believer, every day I must choose to deny my own agenda, deny my own goals (take up my cross), and follow Christ. This means learning to think as He thinks, to love as He loves, to obey as He obeyed, and to hear the will of the Father the way He did. This is accomplished by reading the Scriptures, letting Jesus speak to my heart, and allowing the power of the Holy Spirit to conform my attitudes, goals, and desires to what He knows is best for me.

If you just prayed the prayer above, you can do this, too. After all, the Holy Spirit is now living inside of you. Allow Him to live and move through your hands and feet and to speak through your lips. Pray as Jesus prayed, "Not my will but your will be done" (Matthew 26:39). Tell God that you are willing to do what He wants.

How do we know what God's will is? By reading the Bible, spending time with Him in prayer, and spending time in fellowship with other believers who encourage us and help us grow in our walk with Christ. But it is in our quiet times with Jesus—just Him and us—that we grow the most. We speak to Him through our prayers, and then He speaks back to us. How? In the quietness of our hearts and by making His words come alive to us from the Bible. It is a two-way conversation!

A Transformed Life

As we learn to discern Christ's will, we will see our lives transformed. We will (or should) find ourselves letting go of certain behaviors, such as inappropriate language and actions, and identifying and releasing hidden sins. If we have anger, jealousy, or unforgiveness, we should hand them over to God. If we are controlled by money, we must let God break that stronghold. If we are controlled by the desires of our flesh, we need to let them go.

Giving up our own agendas sounds impossible, and in our own strength, it is. But God never asked us to walk this journey alone. Remember that at the moment of salvation, He gives us the Holy Spirit, who indwells us and gives us power to overcome our failings and temptations. It is the Spirit, God Himself living inside of us, who gives us the power and wisdom we need to become all that He has called us to be. As this happens, we become a better friend, sister, brother, mother, father, child, co-worker, boss, dating partner, and ultimately, spouse.

God bless you as you seek to follow Him and draw closer to Him. You will never regret it!

About the Author

Dr. Emily Edwards is an emerging voice of hope within the field of Christian Counseling. She is a bright, positive, and informed writer and speaker who spends much of her time counseling and helping others in the pursuit, development, and implementation of long-term, meaningful relationships. She frequently travels around the United States, and overseas, leading seminars and retreats for singles, women, and married couples. Edwards received her Ph.D. in Christian Counseling from Vision International University in 2002, along with certifications in pastoral counseling and marriage and family counseling. The scope of her work and ministry includes personal counseling, teaching biblical principles on relationships, and recovery for the hurting.

Notes

Notes

Notes

Notes

Notes

Notes

Notes